Ralf Retter

Theological-Political Resistance

The Role of Dietrich Bonhoeffer and Hans-Bernd von Haeften in the German Resistance against Hitler

Bibliografische Information der Deutschen Nationalbibliothek

Die Deutsche Nationalbibliothek verzeichnet diese Publikation in der Deutschen Nationalbibliografie; detaillierte bibliografische Daten sind im Internet über http://dnb.d-nb.de abrufbar.

ISBN 978-3-8325-2096-0

Logos Verlag Berlin GmbH
Comeniushof, Gubener Str. 47,
10243 Berlin
Tel.: +49 030 42 85 10 90
Fax: +49 030 42 85 10 92
INTERNET: http://www.logos-verlag.de

PREFACE AND ACKNOWLEDGEMENTS

This book is based on a Master's thesis which I submitted in July 2006 at the University of Cambridge in partial fulfilment of the requirements of the M. Phil. Degree in International Relations.

I am very much indebted to my supervisor at Cambridge Dr. Brendan Simms (Peterhouse) for his personal support and his always very helpful comments on the drafts I submitted to him. I would especially like to thank my parents who supported and encouraged me throughout my studies at Cambridge, took the time to read through the thesis and made helpful suggestions.

I also owe much to Trinity College which provided a wonderful intellectual environment as well as great sports, cultural and housing facilities.

I am very grateful to the *Studienstiftung des deutschen Volkes* and the Cambridge European Trust which provided financial support for my studies. Finally, I would like to thank Dr. Volkhard Buchholtz and the *Logos Verlag Berlin* for publishing this work.

Berlin, December 2008

TABLE OF CONTENTS

Introduction 7

Chapter 1. Difference between the political resistance and resistance of the Protestant Church 13

1.1 First layer: Church resistance in order to preserve the institutional independence of the Protestant Church 14

1.2 Second layer: "Barmen" – defending theology 18

1.2.1 Evaluation of the Barmen Declaration 24

1.3 Third layer: Church resistance extending the borders of the church 25

1.4 Conclusion 29

Chapter 2. Dietrich Bonhoeffer's approach to resistance 33

2.1 Distinction from political resistance 34

2.1.1 Immediate reasons for Bonhoeffer's rejection of the Nazi regime 34

2.1.2 Theological motivation for resistance 37

2.2 Distinction from resistance of the Protestant Church 47

2.3 Conclusion 50

Chapter 3. Hans-Bernd von Haeften's approach to resistance........53

3.1 Short biographical notes........56

3.2 Distinction from political resistance........58

3.2.1 Development of Haeften's theological thoughts and his commitment in the Confessing Church........58

Early influences........58
Vienna........61
Bucharest........63

3.2.2 Theological motivation for resistance........69

3.3 Distinction from resistance of the Protestant Church........80

Conclusion........91

Bibliography

Introduction

That there was a German resistance (*Widerstand*) against Hitler is undeniable. What motives and goals it had and how fundamentally it opposed the Nazi regime is, however, still controversial.

The subject of this thesis is the transition from the resistance of the Protestant Church to the political resistance in Nazi Germany. The thesis focuses on the resistance fighters who acted on the borders between the resistance of the Protestant Church and the political resistance and who constitute a link between the two categories of resistance since their actions consisted of elements of both. It concentrates on pastor Dietrich Bonhoeffer and the diplomat Hans-Bernd von Haeften since they are in the author's view the outstanding examples of this phenomenon. It is hypothesized that, in general, we have to distinguish between the resistance of the Protestant Church and the political resistance, and that Haeften's and Bonhoeffer's acts of resistance constitute a synthesis between the two categories.

In the literature we can find a distinction between the political and the church resistance based on the different concepts, motives and goals as well as the means employed by the two forms of resistance.[1] This distinction makes sense since the church resistance differed substantially from the political one. However, in the literature, for example in the works of Hans Mommsen and Klaus-Jürgen Müller, this categorization leads to the attribution of Haeften's activities to the political resistance because of his membership in the Kreisau Circle

[1] See Gerhard Besier, Die Bekennende Kirche und der Widerstand gegen Hitler. Einzelbeobachtungen, *Wort und Dienst*, 18 (1985), 221; see also Peter Steinbach/Johannes Tuchel (eds.), *Widerstand gegen den Nationalsozialismus* (Bonn, 1994), 6.

without, however, sufficiently taking account of his theological motivation. Likewise, Bonhoeffer is regarded as being involved in the resistance of the Confessing Church prior to 1939 and as being a participant in the political resistance since mid-1940.

This thesis, however, argues that Haeften's and Bonhoeffer's activities after 1940 cannot be attributed, as done in the mainstream literature, to the political resistance or be characterized by categories of political resistance such as "national-conservative" *Widerstand* since they were theologically, and not politically, motivated. Nor can their activities be attributed to the church resistance because they aimed at the removal of the Nazi regime and used political means for this purpose. Since, as is explained below, the resistance of the Protestant Church and the political resistance are different categories, and since Bonhoeffer and Haeften cannot be attributed to either category, the thesis argues for an independent category – the theological-political resistance which is characterized by the fact that it is based on the borderline between the resistance of the Protestant Church and the political resistance. The thesis calls Bonhoeffer's and Haeften's approach to resistance "theological-political" resistance, since this term elucidates the theological motivation and political goals and means combined in this category of resistance.

The application of this category helps better understand and is more accurate and appropriate to describe and analyse the motivation and actions of, for example, Bonhoeffer and Haeften than using the classical distinction between the church and the political resistance. Using this category emphasizes that resistance fighters such as Bonhoeffer and Haeften looked at the issue of *Widerstand* primarily through a theological lens and not, as is often suggested in the literature[2], from a political perspective.

Some might argue that the actions of Bonhoeffer and Haeften are also covered by the political resistance, since, to a certain extent, it was inter alia also ethically-religiously motivated. However, this view overlooks the difference between the partly religious motivation of the political resistance and the theological motivation of certain resistance fighters. While religious motivation in the political resistance was based on religious convictions in a general sense, the theological-political resistance was based on a theological-scientific approach to questions related to resistance. Moreover, ethical-religious motives mainly played a role among and besides other motives in the political resistance, were in general only of secondary importance, and only gradually became more significant during the period of the Third Reich. Theological motives, however, were, from the beginning, predominant in the theological-political resistance, and were its main driving force and legitimizing factor for resisting the Nazi regime. Also, while in some cases the resistance activities of representatives of the political resistance, such as Helmut von Moltke, made them faithful, Bonhoeffer's and Haeften's faith made them join the resistance. Moreover, unlike representatives of the political resistance who were inter alia religiously motivated, protagonists of the theological-political resistance, like Bonhoeffer or Haeften, had a background in and were institutionally linked to the Confessing Church, and joined the active resistance also as a result of their involvement in and their critical assessment of actions of the Confessing Church.

---

[2] See, for example, Günther van Norden, Die Barmer Theologische Erklärung und ihr historischer Ort in der Widerstandsgeschichte, in Steinbach/Tuchel (eds.), *Widerstand*, 181.

In the first chapter of the thesis it is explained where the main differences between the resistance of the Protestant Church and the political resistance lie, and why, generally, it indeed makes sense to distinguish between these two categories. For this purpose the thesis distinguishes between and analyses three different layers of church resistance of the Protestant Church. The thesis concentrates on the Confessing Church since it was the main opposition group within the Protestant Church, and points out the particularities of the Confessing Church's approach to *Widerstand* which make it different from the political resistance.

In the second chapter the thesis focuses on Bonhoeffer's approach to resistance and his theological ethics of responsibility. In the author's view Bonhoeffer's approach constitutes, apart from the political and the church resistance, an independent category of resistance, since it is, on the one hand, based on theological motives and the foundations established by the Confessing Church but, on the other hand, goes beyond it and draws political consequences primarily on the basis of Christian faith. Hence, the decision of Bonhoeffer and Haeften to actively plot the killing of Hitler cannot simply be described as going from the church resistance to the political resistance, since, for both, theological motives were still dominant, and since they did not break with their Christian faith but, on the contrary, reconciled their political actions with their religion and received their motivation from their theological thoughts.

It is argued that this category of resistance, which Bonhoeffer described in his own works and of which Bonhoeffer is an example through his own actions, is generally applicable to other resistance fighters. For this purpose the thesis identifies the main features of Bonhoeffer's approach to resistance which are characterized by the fact that the resistance activity was theologically motivated and was looked at from a theological perspective, was a result and extension of activities in the Confessing Church, aimed at the removal of the Nazi regime and used political means for this purpose. These characteristics constitute the criteria of the theological-political resistance.

In the third chapter the thesis applies this concept to Haeften as a case study by analysing his role in the Kreisau Circle and the Confessing Church, his motives to resist, his theological and political positions and his attitude towards the assassination question. The objective is to show how the theological motives, his involvement in the Confessing Church, the political means he used, and the goals he pursued made his activities distinct from the church and the political resistance and similar to Bonhoeffer's approach. The thesis draws the conclusion that there are many similarities between Bonhoeffer's and Haeften's approach to resistance, which justifies subsuming both resistance fighters under the concept of the theological-political resistance.

As opposed to Bonhoeffer, on and by whom we can find a vast amount of publications, there are only few primary and secondary sources relating to Haeften, which have been published or which could be found in the German Foreign Office Archive. Barbara von Haeften, however, compiled her husband's letters, which offer a good insight into his motivation to resist and on which my analysis is primarily based, in a private edition which can be found in the *Gedenkstätte Deutscher Widerstand* (German Resistance Memorial Centre) in Berlin. Since there are many studies on Bonhoeffer but few on Haeften, Haeften's biographical details are looked at in more detail.

The thesis, which analyses theological arguments but, as a historical study, cannot focus on these in detail, only deals with the resistance of the Protestant and not of the Catholic Church because of the institutional, theological and historical differences between the two churches, which would make separate analyses more viable.

In the thesis "resistance" is defined – as in the mainstream literature – as a conscious action against the National Socialist state based on values opposed to Nazi ideology.[3] Hence, for classifying resistance activities, the thesis does not use, also in line with the mainstream literature, Martin Broszat's effectiveness criterion or "functionalist" approach which regards all actions which constituted "a defence, demarcation or restraint to Nazi control independently of the motives and causes"[4] as "*Resistenz*" since this would overstretch and devalue the concept of resistance. Thus, methodologically, the thesis has an "intentionalist" approach asking for the resistance fighters' intentions, i.e. their motivation and goals, and regarding these as the constitutive criteria for the classification of resistance activities and as particularly important for understanding and evaluating the resistance against Hitler. This "intentionalist" method also implies a biographical approach, i.e. a focus on the actions of individual actors.

[3]Peter Steinbach, Der Widerstand als Thema der politischen Zeitgeschichte, in Gerhard Besier/Gerhard Ringshausen (eds.), *Bekenntnis, Widerstand, Martyrium. Von Barmen 1934 bis Plötzensee 1944* (Göttingen, 1986), 32-33.

[4] See Martin Broszat, Resistenz und Widerstand, in Martin Broszat et al. (eds.), *Bayern in der NS-Zeit* (6 vols., Munich, 1977-83), IV. 697.

Chapter 1. Difference between the political resistance and the resistance of the Protestant Church

In this chapter it is argued that the resistance of the Protestant Church and the political resistance which is in the literature predominantly defined as politically motivated resistance aimed at the removal of the Nazi regime[5] cannot be subsumed under one category and have to be distinguished, since the resistance of the Protestant Church differed from the political one in its conception, goals, motives and means. Political resistance had many forms in the Third Reich and ranged from the resistance from the right offered, for example, by conservative groups to the resistance from the left comprising social democratic and communist groups. While political resistance was politically justified and motivated, the resistance of the Protestant Church was guided by theological motives, and constituted a theological conduct and concept. In empirical terms political resistance generally aimed at removing the Nazi regime, whereas the resistance of the Protestant Church was primarily directed at preserving ecclesiastical independence and the religious teachings. While political resistance used political means such as conspiracy and assassination attempts, the Confessing Church especially used indirect means such as memos to resist. Finally, as is shown below, it made a difference whether the issue of resistance was looked at from a theological or a political perspective.

---

[5] See Willibald I. Holzer, *Politischer Widerstand gegen die Staatsgewalt* (Vienna, 1985), 4; Steinbach, *Widerstand als Thema der politischen Zeitgeschichte*, 35.

For the following analysis, which proves the above mentioned hypothesis, three layers of resistance of the Protestant Church are distinguished, i.e. church resistance to preserve the church's institutional independence, to defend the religious teachings, and, finally, church resistance which extended the borders of the church[6]. By looking especially at the motives and goals of the Confessing Church along these three layers, the thesis explains why the resistance of the Confessing Church was not tantamount to political resistance. The chapter focuses on the period before 1940 since, until then, all major decisions which determined and explain the way and attitude of the Confessing Church as a whole towards the Nazi regime throughout the Nazi era had been taken, and since the outbreak of WWII and within this context, Hitler's need to avoid popular unrest in Germany led to a "truce" in the state-church confrontation.[7]

1.1 First layer: Church resistance in order to preserve the institutional independence of the Protestant Church

Church resistance initially formed because of the threat the Nazi regime posed to the independence of the Protestant Church and its attempts to control it through the German Christians.

Within the context of *Gleichschaltung* (coordination), i.e. the effort to bring every level of society under party control, Hitler wanted Germany's 28 regional Lutheran, Reformed and United Churches to be transformed into a unified Evangelical Reich Church in order to bind the Protestant Church to the

[6] See Ernst Wolf, Zum Verhältnis der politischen und moralischen Motive in der deutschen Widerstandsbewegung, in Walter Schmitthenner/Hans Buchheim (eds.), *Der deutsche Widerstand gegen Hitler* (Cologne, 1966), 215-255.

[7] A detailed account of Protestantism in the Nazi era was written by Klaus Scholder, *The Churches and the Third Reich* (2 vols., London 1987-1988) and Kurt Meier, *Der Evangelische Kirchenkampf* (3 vols., Göttingen, 1976-1984).

Third Reich, to rule out any attempts at opposition from this quarter, and to create a counter-balance to the Catholic Church. Since Hitler in the 1920s had decided not to directly intervene in church affairs in order to prevent the NSDAP from entangling in confessional disputes, the task of unifying the *Landeskirchen* (regional churches) was to be carried out by the German Christians, a group within the Protestant Church whose aim it was to adapt Christian faith to Nazi political ideology.

The idea of a united Reich Church born in the 19th century was not a new one, and its realization had always faced opposition in the *Landeskirchen* which enjoyed growing self-consciousness.[8] This time, however, Hitler's plan did not at first meet with much church protest, since there was growing awareness among members of the Protestant Church that the reconstruction and centralisation of the Reich would also necessitate the reconstruction of the church, and that a failure to do so would result in a loss of influence.[9]

When the German Christians, who although they were not pawns of the National Socialists[10] were also used by them to gain control of the Protestant Church, demanded, in line with Nazi ideas and supported by Nazi propaganda, a close relationship between a united Reich Church and the state; the leader principle; the application of the "Aryan paragraph" in the church; and Josef Müller as the Reich Bishop[11], the struggle between the German Christians and the emerging church opposition began, since the latter realized that the independence of the church was at stake. Hence, criticism and protests expressed by the Protestant Church leadership at this

---

[8] Richard Steigmann-Gall, *The Holy Reich. Nazi Conceptions of Christianity, 1919-1945* (Cambridge, 2003), 156.

[9] Meier, *Kirchenkampf*, I. 90.

[10] See Doris L. Bergen, *Twisted Cross* (Chapel Hill, 1996), 4.

[11] Meier, *Kirchenkampf*, I. 109.

stage did not centre on the idea of the Reich Church as such, on theological issues, or on the character of the Nazi regime, but on the threat to the church's independence, i.e. on the questions of what form the Reich Church should have, and who should preside as its Bishop. On the one hand, there was the church administration and leadership which believed that the future Reich Church was to enjoy political and legal independence, and, on the other, there were the German Christians who called for a close legal and practical integration of state and church.

The election of Friedrich von Bodelschwingh, an opponent of the German Christians, as the Reich Bishop designate in May 1933 by representatives from the regional churches in an effort to preserve their independence brought the conflict between the Protestant leadership and the German Christians into the open. While Ludwig Müller, the authorized representative of Hitler for Protestant Church affairs, was nominated by the German Christians in an attempt to create a fait accompli, Friedrich von Bodelschwingh, who was finally elected, was the candidate of the Protestant leadership. The election of Bodelschwingh was of great importance since it demonstrated that the Protestant Church was not willing to give up freedom of decision, at least not in its own sphere.

This, however, challenged Hitler who, not willing to allow church independence and to establish a precedent in the *Gleichschaltung* campaign, decided to impose Müller on the church by force. The NSDAP and Hitler committed themselves to the German Christians with the consequence that Bodelschwingh, faced with the pressure of the German Christians and the NSDAP, had to withdraw his candidacy. Moreover, the German Christians won two thirds of the vote in the church elections to the national synod which approved

Ludwig Müller as the first and only Reich Bishop of the German Evangelical Church.[12]

On 6 September 1933 the national synod also decided to apply the "Aryan paragraph" within the Protestant Church. The "Aryan paragraph" soon became the focal point of early church protests. On 26 September 1933 the Pastor's Emergency League from which the Confessing Church later emerged was founded by Martin Niemöller to help those affected by the application of the paragraph and to oppose the nazification of the church.[13] However, the focus of the Emergency League's protests against the "Aryan paragraph" was not on Jews in general but on the persecution of Jewish Christians, i.e. Jews who had converted to Christianity, given that the application of the paragraph within the church infringed Jewish Christians' confessional freedom, and hence directly affected church members. One of the reasons for this narrow protest was that many church leaders – in line with an interpretation of Luther's doctrine of the two kingdoms to which the thesis will refer below in more detail – believed that the state acted independently and was responsible alone for its decisions. Moreover, the traditional antisemitism and anti-Judaism of the German Protestant Church, which the Pastor Emergency League and Niemöller himself could only partly overcome, also prevented the church from coming to basic decisions and statements on the issue of the persecution of the Jews during the Third Reich.[14]

Hence, concerns about the "Aryan paragraph" were primarily not expressed because of its antisemitic character, but because of the questions it raised about church independence and also

---

[12] See Richard J. Evans, *The Third Reich in power 1933-1939* (London, 2005), 223.

[13] Wolf, *Motive*, 231.

[14] See Günther van Norden, Die Evangelische Kirche und die Juden, *Kirchliche Zeitgeschichte*, 2 (1989), 41.

religious questions which already point to the Protestant Church's second layer of church resistance.

1.2 Second layer: "Barmen" – defending theology

In September 1933 the victory of the German Christians seemed to be complete. They had their man at the head of the Reich Church and controlled – except for the *Landeskirchen* of Bavaria, Württemberg and Hanover – all regional churches. Nevertheless, the Reich Church failed by January 1934, and the Protestant Church could successfully resist an apparently overwhelming church-political power and prevent the coordination of state and church. In this development a new approach formulated by the Swiss professor of theology at Bonn, Karl Barth, was decisive and paved the way for the Barmen Declaration and the beginning of the Confessing Church.

In his work "*Theological Existence Today*", published in July 1933, Barth emphasized that the struggle with the German Christians was not a church-political or political issue but a theological one, and that it therefore had to be fought theologically and not politically.[15] Hence, for Barth the important thing was not to form a centre of church-political resistance but rather a spiritual one. Also, according to Barth, "The Church preaches the Gospel in all the kingdoms of this world. She preaches it also *in* the Third Reich, but not *under* it, nor in *its* spirit."[16] Saying this Barth had found a way of how the Protestant Church could remain a church in the Third Reich and how the German Christian domination of the Protestant Church and the influence of Nazi ideology on the Christian teachings could be opposed. This could be achieved, according to Barth, by the primacy of theology over politics,

[15] Karl Barth, *Theological Existence Today* (London, 1933), 78.

[16] Ibid., 52.

i.e. by interpreting political decisions from a theological point of view and not by interpreting theology from a political viewpoint.[17] Barth came to this view since he wanted to draw a clear line to the politicization of the church, which he believed had contributed to its loss of liberty and independence. This approach constituted a new dimension of church resistance since it did not merely aim at preserving the traditional church institutions but at preserving the liberty of preaching, and of theology and Christian truths in general.
The church opposition adopted Barth's view that the conflict with the German Christians was a theological dispute and not a political one in the "Ulm Declaration" of April 1934 and the "Barmen Declaration" of May 1934, which are regarded as the foundation documents of the Confessing Church.[18]
The delegates to the first Confessing Church synod in Barmen adopted six theses, the Theological Declaration, which clarified the role of the Protestant Church in the confrontation with the German Christians and the state, and established a position of church resistance against the attempts of total *Gleichschaltung* of the church – a position which was specifically theological and not generally political.
The first thesis which, apart from the fifth one, is of particular importance for the topic of the dissertation says that:

> Jesus Christ [...] is the one Word of God, whom we have to hcar, and whom we have to trust and obey in life and in death. We reject the false doctrine that the Church could and should recognize as a source of its proclamation, beyond and besides this one Word of God,

[17] Karl Barth, *Theologische Fragen und Antworten, Gesammelte Vorträge* (Zurich, 1957), 138-141.
[18] Klaus Scholder, *Die Kirchen zwischen Republik und Gewaltherrschaft* (Berlin, 1988), 124.

> yet other events, powers, historic figures and truths as God's revelation.[19]

On the one hand, this was a clear protest against German Christian theology and a rejection of Nazi ideology as a form of revelation. On the other hand, Hans Asmussen, one of the authors of the Declaration, apart from Barth and Thomas Breit, made it explicitly clear in his introductory address at the Barmen Conference presenting the six theses that the problem the first thesis addressed was not just a topical one but a much older question, and that they were not protesting as citizens against the state or the state authorities, but against a phenomenon which had existed for many centuries.[20] For Asmussen as for Barth the errors of the German Christians were a culmination of developments and of a theology which had its origins in the Age of Enlightenment and which interpreted Jesus Christ and the Old and the New Testament as historical events and accepted, apart from the Gospel, also other sources of revelation. At the same time, the first thesis clarified that the struggle with the German Christians was essentially a theological one by referring to Christ as the only authority of the church and by repudiating the teachings of the German Christians. Hence, the Confessing Church had by its own understanding not a political but a theological task and mandate, and as a result of a theological decision did not consider itself a political resistance group.[21]

This approach is confirmed in the fifth thesis in which the fundamental problem of the relationship between state and church is addressed. It says that:

---

[19] Theological Declaration of Barmen (http://www.ucc.org/faith/barmen.htm).

[20] Scholder, *Kirchen*, 127.

[21] Ibid.

> Scripture tells us that by divine appointment the State […] has the task of maintaining justice and peace […] by means of the threat and use of force. The Church acknowledges with gratitude and reverence toward God the benefit of this, his appointment. It draws attention to God's dominion, God's commandment and God's justice, and with these the responsibility of those who rule and those who are ruled […].[22]

This thesis rejected the theological-Christian transfiguration of the state, which had been practiced for centuries, while, at the same time, confirming and acknowledging the state's sovereignty and tasks as well as the right and the justice of state action. But in the repudiation which said that "we repudiate the false doctrine that beyond its special commission the State should and could become the sole and total order of human life"[23] the fifth thesis also reminded the Nazi state of its limits and rejected its totalitarian claim. Hence, "Barmen" clearly distinguishes between state and church, each of which has its own different mandate and its own area of competence and responsibility. While the church possesses an ecclesiastical-theological mandate, the state has a political one.

As far as the question of resistance is concerned, the church, according to Barth, can respond to political challenges for the above mentioned reasons only as church, i.e. could only admonish and had to keep to its sphere, and could not enter the political arena. In short, this would mean that the church, in general, has to obey and recognize the state. If, however, the state adopts, for example, a totalitarian ideology and exceeds its God-given bounds, the church can resist this boundary encroachment in the way of church resistance which because

[22] Theological Declaration.
[23] Ibid.

of its theological basis is a different concept than political resistance.[24]

The Barmen Declaration is, in this sense, also an interpretation of Luther's teaching about a right of resistance and his two-kingdoms doctrine, which, in a nutshell, says that God rules all people in his earthly kingdom through the agency of secular government, i.e. through the law, and all Christians in his spiritual kingdom through the Gospel, thus calling for a proper distinction between the two realms.[25] Luther's distinction between the two kingdoms and its subsequent interpretation, as well as the interpretation of Luther's teaching of a right to resist, contributed to the Confessing Church's passive attitude towards the Nazi regime.

The two-kingdoms doctrine was a way of overcoming the tension between the biblical rules to be, on the one hand, subject to state authorities (Romans 13) and, on the other, to owe God more obedience than to people (Acts 5. 29). For it made clear that Christians in their private life should always obey the Gospel while when holding a public office in the earthly kingdom which was also God's world had to act according to the duties of that office.[26] The tension between the two biblical rules lies at the heart of the teaching of the Christian right of resistance which had been nearly forgotten at the time the Barmen Declaration was issued. As a result of his doctrine of the two kingdoms Luther distinguished between the earthly tyrant who illegitimately usurped or exercised power and the spiritual tyrant who claimed authority

---

[24] Gerhard Ringshausen, Evangelische Kirche und Widerstand, in Huberta Engel (ed.), *Deutscher Widerstand-Demokratie heute: Kirche, Kreisauer Kreis, Ethik, Militär und Gewerkschaften* (Bonn-Berlin, 1992), 71.

[25] See Heinz Eduard Tödt, Die Bedeutung von Luthers Reiche- und Regimentelehre für heutige Theologie und Ethik, in Niels Hasselmann (ed.), *Gottes Wirken in seiner Welt* (2 vols., Hamburg, 1980), II. 101-107.

[26] Hans-Richard Reuter, Widerstandsrecht, in Hans Dieter Betz (ed.), *Religion in Geschichte und Gegenwart* (8 vols., Tübingen, 2005), VIII. 1522-1527.

in the church in violation of God's laws. In such cases there was need for resistance which Luther, however, because of his opinion that membership in the church did not entitle to the use of force initially restricted to passive resistance or "suffering obedience" which required citizens to endure state and church authorities until the utmost limits. After 1530, however, Luther recognized a right of corporate active resistance of the magistrates and princes against the emperor. Luther also described a third type of tyrant, the apocalyptical tyrant or "Anti-Christ", who, on principle, did not recognize the two kingdoms, and exceeded his God-given boundaries. Thereby the tyrant placed himself above and outside God's law, and therefore became, in an eschatological sense, a blasphemer of God, which made active resistance against him a duty.[27]

Given that Luther was more influential in Germany than Calvin or Zwingli, who developed a more radical doctrine of the right to resist, a more restrictive approach to resistance developed in Germany. This restrictive approach was also based on a particular interpretation of Luther's two-kingdoms doctrine. This interpreted the state-church relationship in a dualistic sense in which the political area was thought to be governed by its own inalienable law established by God, with the consequence that all human authority was believed to be ordained by God demanding strict obedience. This interpretation, as well as the rise of legal positivism in the 19th century, made the teaching of the right of resistance practically disappear in Germany, and contributed to the

[27] Johannes Heckel, Widerstand gegen die Obrigkeit, in Johannes Heckel, *Das blinde, undeutliche Wort ‚Kirche'. Gesammelte Aufsätze* (Cologne, 1964), 288-306.

reluctance of the Protestant Church, shown in the Barmen Declaration, to criticize the Third Reich.[28]

1.2.1 Evaluation of the Barmen Declaration

In 1933/1934 the Confessing Church was exclusively concerned with the confession and church order.[29] The Barmen Declaration's realization that the church could and should only react theologically to the challenges posed by the Nazi regime saved the Protestant Church from the *Gleichschaltung* and the German Christians' church-political power. In this theological confrontation the German Christians could not keep up with the Confessing Church. The demand of a primacy of theology over politics and of having a theology, which before making political judgements had reached clarifications about itself, could preserve ecclesiastical independence from the state.
However, the emphasis on church identity and the theological struggle against the German Christians, which excluded a direct political role of the church, came at a price. While "Barmen" protested against the German Christians' theology, no concern was explicitly mentioned about oppression, injustice, violence, concentration camps and the persecution of the Jews, which were questions at issue in May 1934. The delegates to the Barmen synod agreed that no political resistance was intended and left no doubt that, apart from the Nazi church policy, they would be loyal to the state and the *Führer* in all other respect. It therefore seems that the focus on theological disputes and on preserving the independence of the church, as well as the belief that the German Christians were a

[28] See Maier, Recht auf Widerstand, in Steinbach/Tuchel (eds.), *Widerstand*, 36; see also Emanuel Hirsch, Vom verborgenen Souverän, *Glaube und Volk*, Jg. 2 (1933), 4-13; Paul Althaus, *Das Erlebnis der Kirche* (Leipzig, 1924).
[29] Scholder, *Kirchen*, 140.

culmination of a long tradition with origins in the Age of Enlightenment, made the delegates and the Protestant Church, in general, pay little attention to the actual rule of the Nazi regime and to general principles. It is this missing "seventh thesis"[30] which should have spoken against the violation of the law and the persecution of innocent people, which is the major critical point in the Barmen Declaration. And indeed, the Confessing Church, in spite of its fight against the Aryan paragraph, did not realize the scope of Nazi antisemitism.

1.3 Third layer: Church resistance extending the borders of the church

"Barmen", which had determined the boundaries between state and church and the character of the Confessing Church, gave the Confessing Church its direction for the whole period of the Third Reich.[31] It continued its indirect resistance, but split over the question of the relationship and collaboration with the state and in reaction to the new church policy pursued by Hitler after 1935.

In response to the attempts by the Reich Church government to violently seize the *Landeskirchen* of Württemberg and Bavaria and to transform the Reich Church into a single church the Second Confessing Church synod assembled in Berlin-Dahlem in October 1934. At "Dahlem" the Confessing Church broke the relationship with the Reich Church government tied with the state, and on the basis of church emergency law set up its own church leadership, the Councils of Brethren, which were to carry out church government in

[30] Eberhard Bethge, Widerfahrnisse und Umgang mit dem Widertandskomplex, in Eberhard Bethge, *Erstes Gebot und Zeitgeschichte* (Munich, 1991), 173.
[31] Scholder, *Kirchen*, 139.

place of the Reich Bishop and Reich Church government.[32] In line with the Barmen Declaration this meant that the Confessing Church declared itself the only legitimate Protestant Church in Germany. This was a new level of church resistance since the Confessing Church drew the practical consequences of "Barmen" and the policy of the Reich Church, and began to take concrete steps against Hitler's church policy and the German Christians.

"Dahlem" marked the end of the old church policy, whose failure was now evident, and the beginning of a new approach by Hitler. The collapse of the policy of incorporation of the regional churches into the Reich Church with the help of the German Christians and the change in the church-political struggle did not only come about by the domestic political pressure, but also by the external pressure Hitler faced in his church policy.

The struggle of the two churches in Germany became the focus of foreign interest and, alongside the "Jewish question", a heavy burden on German foreign relations. Especially in the United States and Great Britain where Bishop Bell of Chichester, the President of the Ecumenical Council, vehemently protested against the manifest oppression of the Protestant Church in Germany, the state measures against the churches contributed to an anti-German sentiment in the first months of the Third Reich.[33] Since the conflict with the churches worsened the situation of the Reich abroad, and increasingly also became a danger to the implementation of the policy of rearmament, Hitler sacrificed his immediate

---

[32] Shelley Baranowski, *The Confessing Church, Conservative Elites, and the Nazi State* (New York, 1986), 76.

[33] See Conrad Roediger, German Foreign Office Memorandum, 15.10.1934, in *Akten zur deutschen auswärtigen Politik 1918-1945*, C III, 1, 472-473.

plans for the Protestant Church to the more important foreign political interests of the Reich.[34]

In a new approach to settle the church question Hitler tried to put the Protestant Church under state supervision through a policy of "*divide et impera*".[35] The newly appointed minister for church affairs, Hanns Kerrl, established Reich Church Committees in which the different factions of the Protestant Church were to be assembled. They were to replace both the German Christian and the Confessing Church leadership, which had existed in parallel in the regional churches except for the so-called intact *Landeskirchen* Hanover, Württemberg and Bavaria where the German Christians had no stronghold. In other words, the removal of the German Christian leadership was offered as a quid pro quo for the abolition of the Confessing Church.

As a result of this policy the Confessing Church split into a "moderate" group, consisting of the intact *Landeskirchen* led by the Bishops Meiser, Wurm and Marahrens who favoured cooperation with the Reich Church Committees, and the "radical" group of predominantly Prussian Councils of Brethren which rejected the church committee policy, and which elected a new, the so-called, 2nd Provisional Church Government.[36] These divisions did not only relate to the new policy of the Reich government, but also to the broader question of how the Confessing Church viewed itself, and of how Nazism should be best dealt with. Unlike the intact churches, the radical wing of the Confessing Church regarded the Confessing Church as the only legitimate church in Germany and did not recognize the Reich Church Committees as the church government, since this would have implied abandoning this claim.

---

[34] Scholder, *Churches*, 264.
[35] Ringshausen, *Widerstand*, 72.
[36] Scholder, *Kirchen*, 142.

Also, while representatives of the intact churches believed that working within the system could prevent worse developments, and would help the Confessing Church, the church resistance which the more radical members of the Confessing Church – represented by the 2nd Provisional Church Government – pursued, was one of a new quality since it extended the borders of the church by resisting the Nazi state in a broader sense.

The strongest expression of the new attitude towards the state was the so-called Hitler Memo, i.e. a letter addressed to Hitler, drafted by the Provisional Church Government in May 1936. It criticised the attacks of the state against the Christian, the state intervention in church affairs, the National Socialist ideology, the deification of Hitler and the totalitarian structure of the Nazi state, and explicitly objected to antisemitism and the growing persecution of the Jews as well as the disrespect for the rule of law in general.[37] The memo indicated that some Confessing Christians finally recognized that not the German Christians were the real threat to the church but the Nazi state and Nazism. The realization of this threat was difficult because of the previous focus of the Confessing Church's struggle on the German Christians, and because of the fact that the state officially took a neutral stand in this confrontation. In short, in the memo, the Protestant Church protested for the first time vigorously against the state authorities on issues which extended the borders of the church.[38]

However, since the 2nd Provisional Church Government put the politically charged issues into a specifically church-related context, it avoided direct political resistance. Moreover, the church leaders did not publicize the letter, but sent it privately

[37] Martin Greschat (ed.), *Zwischen Widerspruch und Wahrheit. Texte zur Denkschrift der Bekennenden Kirche an Hitler* (Munich, 1987), 152-160.
[38] Wolf, *Motive*, 237.

to Hitler himself.[39] This indirectness, which made public discussions and awareness of the injustice in Nazi Germany impossible, as well as the Confessing Church's passive attitude, remained unchanged during WWII.

1.4 Conclusion

The resistance of the Protestant Church increased, corresponding to the sharpening of the Nazi terror and along the three layers of resistance which have been distinguished above.

In 1933 the Protestant Church approved of the Nazi regime. Scepticism about the Weimar Republic, the traditional respect for authority, and the nationalist sentiment and extremely conservative tradition of German Protestantism contributed to the church's wish to participate in the national "awakening", and prevented it from disapproving of, let alone, resisting Hitler in early 1933.[40] The Nazi church policy, which wanted to pursue a policy of *Gleichschaltung* with regard to the churches and sought to control the Protestant Church through the German Christians, forced the church to react. Being challenged in its independence the church opposition to the German Christians chose its own candidate for the Reich Bishop, but eventually had to back down after Hitler's intervention.

The Barmen Declaration was another layer of resistance since it protested against the German Christians' theology. This protest, however, had no direct political dimension, since it was confined to the religious realm, and since it did not put into question the general loyalty to the National Socialist rule.

[39] Ringshausen, *Widerstand*, 74-75.

[40] See Manfred Gailus, *Protestantismus und Nationalsozialismus. Studien zur nationalsozialistischen Durchdringung des protestantischen Sozialmilieus in Berlin* (Cologne, 2001), 638-640.

Nevertheless, since the NSDAP did not recognize the theological difference between the political and the church resistance, and was not willing to allow a challenge to its monopoly on ideological rule, the Confessing Church became a "resistance movement against its will"[41]. Hence, "Barmen" and the Confessing Church in emphasizing their ecclesiastical-theological intentions and in their struggle against the Nazi church policy had an indirect political effect, and signalled at least potential opposition to the Nazi regime.
After 1936 the resistance of the Confessing Church became more direct, since it protested against the violation of human rights in general, and not only against the violation of church rights, realizing that the real threat was the Nazi regime and not the German Christian movement. The Confessing Church began to attack the essential characteristics of the Nazi regime, i.e. its totalitarian claims. It attacked National Socialism as a political religion and thus its very nature by rejecting and contesting the Nazi state's claim to become the total order of human life. Hence, the Confessing Church's approach to resistance contained the theological seeds of broader resistance. Moreover, through its connections with foreign countries it informed the world of the events that took place in Germany. Since these were conscious actions against the Nazi regime, it is at least justified speaking of an approach of "resistance" of the Confessing Church. Altogether, however, this was not political but church resistance since the Confessing Church's overwhelming majority at no time and by its own understanding aimed at the removal of the Nazi regime, did not use political means such as conspiracy and violent actions, differed fundamentally in its motivation from those involved in the political resistance and conceived of their actions as an ecclesiastical concept and conduct as opposed to the political resistance.

---

[41] Wolf, *Motive*, 219.

Because of the above mentioned empirical and conceptual differences, the resistance of the Confessing Church and the political resistance have to be distinguished. In a summarizing definition, confirmed by the academic writings[42], the resistance of the Protestant Church was a theologically motivated opposition to the Nazi regime, which primarily aimed at the preservation of church independence and of the religious teachings. As opposed to church resistance the political resistance against Hitler is defined by the academic writings[43], in line with the "intentionalist" approach, as a politically motivated opposition to the National Socialist regime aimed at its removal, and based predominantly on basic political convictions using political means. This definition rejects a very broad and general understanding of political resistance which would regard all acts of resistance in Nazi Germany which made use of political means as political resistance. This would be an inadequate understanding overstretching the political resistance concept since the means used in the resistance only helped materialize the broader aims and ideas of the resistance fighters and, hence, can only be one criterion for categorizing resistance activities.

If the distinction between the resistance of the Protestant Church and the political resistance on the basis of the above mentioned characteristics is indeed useful, and if political resistance is mainly understood as politically motivated

---

[42] See Günther van Norden, Widerstand im deutschen Protestantismus 1933-1945, in Christoph Klessmann/Falk Pingel (eds.), *Gegner des Nationalsozialismus* (Frankfurt am Main, 1980), 104; Robert P. Ericksen, Resistance in the German Protestant Church, in Francis R. Nicosia/Lawrence D. Stokes (eds.), *Germans against Nazism*, 120.

[43] See Holzer, *Widerstand*, 4; Steinbach, *Widerstand als Thema der politischen Zeitgeschichte*, 35.

resistance, the question, however, is how Bonhoeffer's and Haeften's approach to resistance have to be classified.

Chapter 2. Dietrich Bonhoeffer's approach to resistance

The distinction between the political resistance and the resistance of the Protestant Church leads in the literature to the attribution of Bonhoeffer's activities after mid-1940 to the political resistance in order to emphasize the differences to the church resistance.
In the following chapter, however, it is argued that Bonhoeffer's approach to resistance is distinct both from the political resistance in the sense of politically motivated resistance and the resistance of the Protestant Church. One might say that it constituted the fourth layer of the Protestant Church's church resistance, i.e. the active resistance of the Protestant Church directed at the removal of the Nazi regime. However, since the Confessing Church did not follow Bonhoeffer's approach and disapproved of it, which is demonstrated by the fact that it refused to place his name on the intercession lists after Bonhoeffer's arrest[44], it is more appropriate to consider Bonhoeffer's approach as an independent category of resistance. The thesis justifies this assessment by distinguishing Bonhoeffer's resistance from the political resistance and the resistance of the Protestant Church and by outlining its most important characteristics. For this purpose Bonhoeffer's reasons for his rejection of the Nazi regime and his motivation for joining the resistance are initially analysed. Afterwards the thesis examines the main characteristics of his acts of resistance.

[44] Eberhard Bethge, *Dietrich Bonhoeffer. Christian. Theologian. Man for his Times* (Minneapolis, 2000), 794.

2.1 Distinction from political resistance

Regarding Bonhoeffer's resistance after mid-1940 as political resistance[45] and simply characterizing it with categories of political resistance by describing it as "liberal-conservative"[46] or "national-conservative"[47] as done in the literature is, in the author's view, inappropriate and misleading since it would neglect and ignore the primary importance of Bonhoeffer's theological thoughts in his resistance activities. This theological approach gives Bonhoeffer's resistance a particular character, making it a link and transition between the resistance of the Protestant Church and the political resistance. Bonhoeffer (04.02.1906-09.04.1945)[48] in 1940 did not simply join the political resistance, leaving theology behind him. On the contrary, his active resistance was reflected in his theological thinking and writing, and arose out of Christian positions and not of political considerations.

2.1.1 Immediate reasons for Bonhoeffer's rejection of the Nazi regime

There were mainly four motives – the destruction of the constitutional state, the state-church conflict, Hitler's warmongering and Nazi antisemitism – which made Bonhoeffer reject the Nazi movement and regime from the

---

[45] See van Norden, *Barmer Theologische Erklärung*, 181.

[46] See Christoph Strohm, *Theologische Ethik im Kampf gegen den Nationalsozialismus. Der Weg Dietrich Bonhoeffers mit den Juristen Hans von Dohnanyi und Gerhard Leibholz in den Widerstand* (Munich, 1989), 346.

[47] See Klaus-Jürgen Müller, Nationalkonservative Elite zwischen Kooperation und Widerstand, in Jürgen Schmädecke/Peter Steinbach (eds.), *Der Widerstand gegen den Nationalsozialismus* (Munich-Zurich, 1985), 24-49; Hans Mommsen, Der Widerstand gegen Hitler und die deutsche Gesellschaft, in Schmädecke/Steinbach (eds.), *Widerstand*, 3-23.

[48] See Bethge, *Bonhoeffer* for a detailed account of Bonhoeffer's life.

beginning of the 1930s.[49] All of these motives had a theological context and were regarded by Bonhoeffer predominantly from a theological perspective.

For Bonhoeffer and his friends and family circle Hitler meant war. Bonhoeffer realized, also thanks to his studies at the Union Theological Seminary in New York (1930-1931) and his commitment in the ecumenical movement, that the churches of different countries could never solely be national churches because of their adherence to the one Jesus Christ, and were ecumenically attached to one another. This, and his discovery of and identification with the biblical message of peace of the Sermon on the Mount, at the beginning of the 1930s, made him demand from the church a commitment for peace and understanding among nations, and made him fight for a theological proscription of war.[50] Bonhoeffer's theologically justified opposition to war was one major reason for his fight against National Socialism.

Another reason was Nazi antisemitism and the persecution of the Jews by the Third Reich. Bonhoeffer justified the rejection of the Nazi treatment of Jews as such and not merely of baptized Jews in his article "*The Church and the Jewish Question*"[51] by the role and limits of the state authority within the context of the two-kingdoms doctrine and the salvation-historical role of the Jewish people and thus by a theological argumentation. Bonhoeffer regarded the "Jewish question" not as a biological or racial issue, but as a religious one. In the above mentioned article he argued that the church would cease

---

[49] Heinz Eduard Tödt, Der Bonhoeffer-Dohnanyi-Kreis in der Opposition und im Widerstand gegen das Gewaltregime Hitlers, in Christian Gremmels/Ilse Tödt (eds.), *Internationales Bonhoeffer Forum 7* (Munich, 1987), 215.

[50] Tödt, Bonhoeffer-Dohnanyi-Kreis, 212; see also Eberhard Bethge, Dietrich Bonhoeffers Weg vom „Pazifismus" zur Verschwörung, in Hans Pfeifer (ed.), *Internationales Bonhoeffer Forum 5* (Munich, 1982), 121.

[51] Dietrich Bonhoeffer, The Church and the Jewish Question, in Dietrich Bonhoeffer, *Selected Writings* (London, 1995), 45-47.

to remain church if it limited its solidarity with the Jewish Christians and allowed the state to exclude them from the church. In respect of the discrimination of non-baptised Jews, Bonhoeffer demanded the church's full solidarity with them since it was the church's duty to help the victims of state action. According to Bonhoeffer, the task of the state given it by God was to create law and order. Consequently, depriving Jewish citizens of their rights as full and equal citizens would mean that the state exercised "too little law and order"[52], which would constitute illegitimate governmental action.[53] Although *The Church and the Jewish Question* also contained much conservative views on the theological role of the Jewish people, Bonhoeffer later unequivocally argued that the Jews were "the brothers of Jesus Christ"[54], and indissolubly linked to Christian identity, with the consequence that "an expulsion of the Jews from the West must necessarily bring with it the expulsion of Christ; for Christ was a Jew"[55]. This leaves no doubt that Nazi antisemitism motivated him to a great extent to reject the Nazi regime.

Bonhoeffer's rejection of the destruction of the rule of law was certainly also a result of political considerations and a general political attitude which opposed dictatorial rule. But also with regard to this question, Bonhoeffer had a theological perspective, since the tasks of the state set by the two-kingdoms theory and given by God became the yardstick for Bonhoeffer to judge the existence of the rule of law in Nazi Germany. In his article on the "Jewish question" Bonhoeffer

[52] Bonhoeffer, *Jewish Question*, 47.

[53] See Heinz Eduard Tödt, Judendiskriminierung 1933- der Ernstfall für Bonhoeffers Ethik, in Wolfgang Huber/Ilse Tödt (eds.), *Internationales Bonhoeffer Forum 4* (Munich, 1982), 170-171.

[54] Dietrich Bonhoeffer, Confession of Guilt, in Dietrich Bonhoeffer, *Ethics* (London, 1993), 93.

[55] Bonhoeffer, *Ethics*, 70.

spoke about “a group of men”[56] in a general sense whose deprivation of civil rights would mean that the state exercised “too little order”. Hence, given that the Nazi regime, for example, also made Communists and other groups of persons lawless, Bonhoeffer must have been convinced that the National Socialist state in general exercised “too little law and order” and thereby destroyed the rule of law.
Finally, the attempts of the German Christians and the Nazi regime to dominate and nazify the Protestant Church showed Bonhoeffer that National Socialism did not recognize the boundaries between state and church, and that its political messianism with its pseudo-religious claims[57] inevitably had to come into conflict with the Christian religion and its understanding of governmental tasks.[58]
In short, Bonnhoeffer’s immediate reasons to reject the Nazi regime, analysed above, predominantly arose out of a theological and not a political context and perspective. However, these motives did not automatically pave the way for Bonhoeffer’s resistance, given that there were difficult theological problems to overcome and theological insights to be found, and consequences to be drawn from his rejection of the Nazi regime before the decision to join the resistance could be taken. In the following part, his motivation to take part in the active resistance will, therefore, be analysed.

2.1.2 Theological motivation for resistance

That his decision to contribute to the plans for a coup did not arise out of political calculations but out of his theological

---

[56] Bonhoeffer, *Jewish Question*, 48.
[57] On this issue see Claus-Ekkehard Bärsch, *Die politische Religion des Nationalsozialismus* (Munich, 1998).
[58] Christoph Strohm, „Zweireichelehre“ und antiliberales Rechtsverständnis bei Bonhoeffer?, *Kirchliche Zeitgeschichte*, 1 (1988), 265.

reasoning and his experience with and critical assessment of the resistance of the Confessing Church, is shown by his article on the "Jewish Question" and the "*Confession of Guilt*"[59], which he wrote in autumn 1940, at the time that he joined the conspiracy.

As early as 1933 Bonhoeffer had argued against the conventional belief in the apolitical character of the church, and demanded an active role of it when he made a public statement on the discrimination against the Jews in the *The Church and the Jewish Question*. Although he still emphasized the boundaries between the state and the church, in line with the two-kingdoms doctrine, when, for example, writing that the church could not, in the first place, act as a direct political agent and that state actions should remain free from church intervention[60], Bonhoeffer in the same document also came to more far-reaching views. This becomes evident when he says that the church has three possible ways it can act against the state: First, the church must ask the state if its actions are legitimate. Second, the church owes help and service to every victim of any social order, regardless of his or her religious confession. "The third possibility is that when the church sees the state exercising too little or too much law and order, it is its task not simply to bind the wounds of the victims beneath the wheel, but to put a spoke in the wheel itself."[61] Bonhoeffer, however, did not intend that the recognition of the third possibility of how the church could act against the state, i.e. that of active resistance, should be left to the decision of the individual; it was to be carried out and

[59] Bonhoeffer, *Confession of Guilt*, 89-95.

[60] Bonhoeffer, *Jewish Question*, 47; see also Eberhard Bethge, Dietrich Bonhoeffer und die theologische Begründung seines politischen Widerstandes, in Eberhard Bethge, *Am gegebenen Ort. Aufsätze und Reden* (Munich, 1979), 56.

[61] Bonhoeffer, *Jewish Question*, 48.

authorized by an "Evangelical Council".[62] Only after his disappointment about the missing corporate resistance from the church did Bonhoeffer in 1938 conclude that to "put a spoke in the wheel" could also be the result of individual decision. He, however, did not abandon his concept that the church as a whole should resist, but argued that there were two "Christian" ways of resistance which existed in parallel, the resistance of the church and of individual Christians.[63] His belief that the church could directly act politically was opposed to Barth's early views on this issue, which he only changed in 1938 after he had left Germany. Bonhoeffer was aware that direct political action of the church would jeopardize its existence. However, he also increasingly realized that the view that the church could remain neutral and apolitical was a fiction since abstaining from politics in the face of the totalitarian character of the Nazi regime inevitably included a political message and was, in fact, impossible, because of the church's political and social role in German society. Moreover, Bonhoeffer was convinced that the church could not keep away from the world but had to bear witness and had to act in real life. Bonhoeffer's *Confession of Guilt*, inter alia, confesses that:

> The Church was silent when she should have cried out because the blood of the innocent was crying aloud to heaven [...]. The Church confesses that she has witnessed the lawless application of brutal force, the physical and spiritual suffering of countless innocent people [...]. She is guilty of the deaths of the weakest and most defenceless brothers of Jesus Christ [i.e. the Jews].[64]

---

[62] Eberhard Bethge, *Bonhoeffer. An Illustrated Biography* (New York, 1979), 40.
[63] Strohm, *Ethik*, 333.
[64] Bonhoeffer, *Ethics*, 92-93.

This statement indicates that Bonhoeffer wanted the church to play a more active role in resisting the Nazi regime and that he refused the Confessing Church's "confessing approach", i.e. the rejection of active resistance and the concentration on the confessional work in order to protect the church from the influences of Nazi ideology and to keep Christian faith pure.

The *Confession of Guilt* also suggests that Bonhoeffer regarded his own activity as the one demanded by the church and as a conduct carried out in place of the church. Hence, for Bonhoeffer, the necessity to join the active resistance and thus the necessity to accept guilt resulted from the missing assumption of responsibility by the Protestant Church.[65]

Bonhoeffer's decision to join the resistance was also made possible by his theological interpretation of the Nazi regime. Bonhoeffer used an apocalyptical characterization of the Third Reich, and thereby put it into a theological context. For example, in September 1941 Bonhoeffer warned that "it has become increasingly difficult for the German nation to understand the true character of the regime, and that relatively few have remained unshaken in their conviction that it represented Satan masquerading as an Angel of Light"[66]. Moreover, in July/August 1940 he referred, according to Bishop Bell, to Hitler as the "Anti-Christ" who is a person in the biblical apocalypse embodying evil.[67] Resistance was not only possible but required – this must have been Bonhoeffer's conclusion as is shown below – if Hitler represented evil.

---

[65] Bethge, *Begründung*, 52; Andreas Pangritz, Dietrich Bonhoeffers theologische Begründung der Beteiligung am Widerstand, *Evangelische Theologie*, 55 (1995), 507-508.

[66] Dietrich Bonhoeffer, The Church and the new order in Europe, in Dietrich Bonhoeffer, *Gesammelte Schriften* (4 vols., Munich, 1956), I. 366.

[67] George Bell, The background of the Hitler plot, in Bonhoeffer, *Gesammelte Schriften*, I. 397; according to Bethge, however, this is improbable, see Bethge, *Bonhoeffer*, 722.

Bonhoeffer deals with and analyses from a theological perspective the issue of resistance and its related questions in his posthumously published work *Ethics* which gives us an important insight into this matter since Bonhoeffer wrote it between the time he joined the conspiracy and the time he was arrested (1940-1943).[68] Bonhoeffer's ethics is a theological ethics of responsibility since its central theme is responsible action. Bonhoeffer argues that responsible life is conditioned by two factors: First, it is conditioned by the bond of life to man and God which includes deputyship, i.e. the responsibility to act in place and on behalf of others, and the correspondence to reality. Second, it is conditioned by the freedom of a person's own life, which materializes in the venture of a concrete decision, the risk of failure, and the acceptance of guilt.[69]

For Bonhoeffer, Christian rules correspond to reality, and the role of the church is to speak the word of God concretely from its knowledge of the matter, and not to proclaim general principles which are always true.[70] Consequently, Bonhoeffer opposes any retreat into the private sphere since, according to him, any attempt to avoid personal guilt and any attempt to preserve moral purity by withdrawing from conflicts is morally irresponsible and has nothing to do with Christ or Christianity, given that, according to Bonhoeffer, responsible action is founded in the reality of God and the reality of the world reconciled in Christ.[71]

Bonhoeffer's *Ethics* is a "situation ethic"[72], the meaning of which becomes clear when Bonhoeffer writes that the conduct

---

[68] Traugott Jähnichen, Freie Verantwortlichkeit und Zivilcourage, in Günther Brakelmann/Traugott Jähnichen (eds.), *Dietrich Bonhoeffer- Stationen und Motive auf dem Weg in den politischen Widerstand* (Münster, 2005), 101.

[69] Bonhoeffer, Ethics, 194.

[70] Ibid., 66-67.

[71] Jähnichen, *Freie Verantwortung*, 101.

[72] See Bethge, *Begründung*, 61.

of the responsible man is not established in advance as a matter of principle, but arises with the given situation. Nobody knows whether one realizes good in history according to God's aims since all attempts to define that which is good once and for all always ends in failure. As a result responsible action aims at the venture of an own decision and is in this sense a free venture of faith. The judgement about the deed and its consequences is entirely delivered to God.[73] Since responsible action finds its reference point in Christ on whom reality is founded and tries to respond to divine call, it can refrain from any form of self-justification.

In *Ethics* Bonhoeffer realizes that everyone who acts responsibly becomes guilty, and that anyone trying to escape guilt in responsibility detaches him- or herself from the ultimate reality of human existence.[74] In other words, Bonhoeffer regards the feeling of guilt resulting from abstaining from active resistance as more intolerable than the one related to active resistance and, hence, also to violent means for which he was ready to take personal responsibility before God. Since it is always a venture to recognize what is "right" to do, given that it is not established in advance, but must be seen in a given situation, the action of the responsible person must be linked to God's forgiveness for sins.[75]

These thoughts make clear that for Bonhoeffer resistance against Hitler was the venture of faith as an assumption of responsibility in the hope for forgiveness by God and vicarious representative action. In the case of extraordinary situations of ultimate necessities, for example when state authorities destroy the fundamental orders that structure human life and dissolve the legal order, Bonhoeffer highlights the necessity of vicarious representative action and the free

[73] Bonhoeffer, Ethics, 197.

[74] Ibid., 210.

[75] Ibid., 209-210.

responsibility of the individual even if his or her actions are not covered by the applicable law. Free responsibility of the individual can thus include the complete renunciation of the applicable law since "the law is no longer the last thing, there is still Jesus Christ."[76]

These theological ideas of *Ethics* paved the way for Bonhoeffer's active resistance, since for Bonhoeffer – because of his responsibility and the concrete situation which demanded responsible action – the participation in the resistance was the only possible option he could choose as a Christian in view of the Nazi regime. In Bonhoeffer's view, the failure to resist the Nazi state was tantamount to condoning evil given that, faced with this situation, there was no middle path or escape from responsibility in the form of turning away from the world for the above mentioned reasons.[77]

Bonhoeffer's thoughts on resistance and responsible life contained in *Ethics* were remarkable since, as shown above, the theory of religious resistance, although not lacking in Luther, had become obscured in Germany by the historical development of German Protestantism and the age of legal positivism.[78] Also, in *Ethics* Bonhoeffer – with his realization that the reality of the world and of God are reconciled in Christ – overcomes the neo-Lutheran interpretation of the two-kingdoms theory which, according to him, had led the church to neglect its political responsibility. He does not give up the teaching that God rules the world through the spiritual office and the secular government and that each of them has its own responsibility.[79] However, the two kingdoms, according to

---

[76] Ibid., 216.

[77] Sabine Dramm, *Dietrich Bonhoeffer. Eine Einführung in sein Denken* (Gütersloh, 2001), 211.

[78] Hans Rothfels, *The German opposition to Hitler* (London, 1962), 39.

[79] Bethge, *Begründung*, 57.

Bonhoeffer, shall not be thought of as static antitheses, serving to designate certain mutually exclusive entities since this would fail to recognize the unity of the two realms accomplished in Christ.[80] Instead, the two kingdoms do not exist in themselves or on their own account but adopt "a polemic attitude towards each other" and "have to prevent one another from assuming any kind of static independence in their mutual relations."[81] Hence, Bonhoeffer protests against a Christianity which detaches itself from the earthly reality, and against the neo-Protestant tendency of sanctifying the world and of regarding it as being autonomous. In short, Bonhoeffer therefore rejects the view that the doctrine of the two kingdoms implies a duty for Christians to abstain from political action and to pay uncritical obedience to state authorities.

His own perception of his activities also indicates that he did not regard himself as exercising genuine political resistance, since he said, for example, in a letter from the end of 1943, addressed to his parents, that "you must know that I have not for a moment regretted coming back in 1939 – nor any of the consequences, either. I knew quite well what I was doing, and I acted with a clear conscience."[82] In another letter he said that "I became certain that it was my duty to endure this borderline case [German: *Grenzfall*] with all its problems."[83] The term "borderline case" describes very well his situation. While Bonhoeffer was an employee of the *Abwehr* and involved in the preparations for the plot against Hitler, he remained in the service of the Confessing Church and worked for the Confessing Church as a theological adviser at the same time. Moreover, Bonhoeffer's involvement in the conspiracy did not

[80] Bonhoeffer, *Ethics*, 170.

[81] Ibid.

[82] Dietrich Bonhoeffer, *Letters and Papers from Prison* (New York, 1997), 174.

[83] Ibid., 129.

reduce his solidarity with the fate of the Confessing Church. Although he had sharply criticized the Confessing synods, and although the Confessing Church could no longer identify itself with Bonhoeffer's cause, the Confessing Church remained Bonhoeffer's church.[84] Therefore, Bonhoeffer can be conceived of as one of the few of the Confessing Church who took the step of active resistance, while the mainstream Confessing Church was not able to think in the categories which Bonhoeffer believed to be necessary to respond to the extraordinary demand of the situation.[85] Bonhoeffer's statements that "I have not for a moment regretted coming back in 1939 – nor any of the consequences, either" and that "I acted with a clear conscience"[86] in addition show that his participation in the resistance was in conformity with his theology and not opposed to it.

Bonhoeffer's particular approach to resistance had consequences for the way he acted in the resistance and how he viewed the situation of Germany.

For example, when Visser't Hooft asked Bonhoeffer in September 1941 during his second Swiss journey for what he was praying, Bonhoeffer answered – at a time when Germany seemed to win the war – that "I pray for the defeat of my country, for I think it is the only possibility of atoning for all the suffering that my country has caused in the world."[87] Also, according to Bishop Bell's account of his meeting with Bonhoeffer in Sweden in May 1942, Bonhoeffer saw the necessity of a "punishment by God" for Germany and regarded the conspiracy as "an act of repentance".[88] In this attitude Bonhoeffer differed from most other resistance

---

[84] Bethge, *Bonhoeffer*, 686.

[85] Ibid., 794.

[86] Bonhoeffer, *Letters*, 174.

[87] Dietrich Bonhoeffer, *Dietrich Bonhoeffers Werke* 16 (Gütersloh, 1996), 751.

[88] Statements made by Bonhoeffer according to George Bell, The Church and the Resistance Movement, in Bonhoeffer, *Gesammelte Schriften*, I. 405

fighters since, first, Bonhoeffer did not refuse an unconditional surrender[89] and, hence, also accepted a loss of Germany's great power status as opposed to those who strove to maintain at least some of Hitler's territorial gains after a coup. Second, his statements show again that for Bonhoeffer political considerations such as questions of power did not play any significant role for his motivation to resist and that he conceived of the German resistance in terms of theological concepts such as repentance and atonement. For Bonhoeffer, the planned coup had a theological significance and had to take place as part of the "punishment by God" and had thus to be recognized as the Germans' acceptance of guilt and repentance.[90]

Another example of how Bonhoeffer's theological approach influenced his actions is the so-called "Operation 7" by which Bonhoeffer and Dohnanyi in September 1942 could rescue 14 Jews by sending them as "spies" to Switzerland. After the war Hans-Bernd Gisevius, a conspirator in the *Abwehr*, argued that the operation had put at risk the planned coup and had diverted the *Abwehr* from the overall goal of overthrowing the Nazi regime.[91] This is the view one can assume if Bonhoeffer is considered to be a conspirator of the political resistance. "Operation 7", however, can only be properly understood if its theological dimension, which consisted in the practical Christian solidarity exercised by Bonhoeffer and Dohnanyi and the importance they attributed to each human life, is not neglected.

---

[89] See Pangritz, *theologische Begründung*, 510.

[90] Klemens von Klemperer, *German resistance against Hitler: the search for allies abroad, 1938-1945* (Oxford, 1994), 286.

[91] Ibid., 517; see Hans-Bernd Gisevius, *Bis zum bitteren Ende* (2 vols., Zurich 1946), II. 267.

2.2 Distinction from resistance of the Protestant Church

Bonhoeffer's resistance cannot be conceived of as church resistance, either. While the Confessing Church did not seek to overthrow the Nazi regime and viewed its purpose, as a Christian Church, as helping those, in Bonhoeffer's words "under the wheel", Bonhoeffer decided that his duty was to go beyond this and to oppose the Nazi regime in general.[92] This objective combined with his theological motivation and his background in the Confessing Church make Bonhoeffer a link between the resistance of the Protestant Church and the political resistance.

At the beginning of the Third Reich Bonhoeffer generally conformed to the restrictive approach of the Confessing Church, and focused on opposing *Gleichschaltung* in the ecclesiastical area. For example, by contributing in summer 1933 to the creation of the "Bethel Confession" which became a forerunner of the Barmen Declaration, Bonhoeffer took part in the efforts of the emerging Confessing Church to lay down their confession in order to combat distortions.[93] Also, in 1935 Bonhoeffer began his work as head of the illegal seminary for Confessing Church pastors in Finkenwalde. This seminary was independent from the state and a result of the decision of "Dahlem" to establish emergency church bodies, which shows that Bonhoeffer, generally, conformed to the line of the Confessing Church in this respect. Moreover, in his work "*The Cost of Discipleship*" (1937), which he wrote during his time in Finkenwalde, he says that "The only way to overcome evil is to let it run its course, so that it does not find the resistance it is looking for. Resistance merely creates further evil and adds fuel to the flames."[94] This statement makes clear that he

---

[92] Barnett, *Seoul*, 181.

[93] Bethge, *Illustrated biography*, 41.

[94] Dietrich Bonhoeffer, *The Cost of Discipleship* (London, 1948), 122.

was generally in line with the Confessing Church's rejection of active and direct resistance in the early years of the Nazi era. As shown in *Ethics*, however, Bonhoeffer left these orthodox attitudes and later embraced less doctrinaire views.

The theological convictions, insights and motives mentioned above led Bonhoeffer to dissociate himself from the apolitical viewpoint of the Confessing Church and to join in fall 1940 a resistance circle in the *Abwehr* (German military intelligence), formed around Hans von Dohnanyi, Hans Oster and Wilhelm Canaris, head of the *Abwehr*. This resistance circle to which Bonhoeffer belonged wanted to overthrow the National Socialist regime by killing Hitler and prepared a coup and the assassination of the *Führer*.

Bonhoeffer thus became an active participant in the resistance. The literature considers Bonhoeffer since 1938 as an accessory to plans to overthrow Hitler – Bonhoeffer was informed by talks with his brother-in-law Hans von Dohnanyi who was, from the beginning, involved in these plans – and since summer[95] or fall 1940[96] as an active conspirator.[97]

Disguised as a civil employee of the *Abwehr* in the position of a "confidential agent", Bonhoeffer undertook trips to Switzerland, Sweden, Norway and Italy between 1941 and 1943, which had been made possible by *Abwehr* commissions. Bonhoeffer made these trips on behalf of the German resistance, i.e. not only on behalf of the conspirators in the *Abwehr* but also of the Kreisau Circle. On these trips Bonhoeffer informed foreign friends about the continuing existence and work of the German resistance and brought back

[95] See Bethge, *Bonhoeffer*, 722

[96] See Dramm, *Einführung*, 208.

[97] Andreas Pangritz even interprets Bonhoeffer's return from America in July 1939 as a decision to participate in the conspiracy, see Pangritz, *theologische Begründung*, 501.

information from abroad.[98] Bonhoeffer could especially use his ecumenical contacts with British church leaders and other clergymen in order to discover from Churchill under which conditions Germany could expect to obtain peace with the Allies in the wake of a successful coup.[99] For example, he met Visser't Hooft, secretary general of the provisional World Council of Churches, during his first (February/March 1941) and second trip (August/September 1941) to Switzerland and alerted him to the state-church conflict and the existence of the "euthanasia" programme in Germany. In Sweden in May 1942 Bonhoeffer met Bishop Bell to whom he gave precise details of an impending putsch in order to convince the British government of the earnestness of the conspiracy.[100]

Moreover, Bonhoeffer also participated in discussions about the reorganization of the German state, society and economy. In 1942 on behalf of the Provisional Church Government of the Confessing Church Bonhoeffer made contact with the so-called Freiburg Circle which comprised, among others, the economist Constantin von Dietze and the historian Gerhard Ritter. The circle discussed the reorganization of Germany and was invited by Bonhoeffer to develop recommendations which were to be presented after the war at an ecumenical conference (the so-called Freiburg memorandum).[101] Also, Bonhoeffer had contacts with the Kreisau Circle, thanks to his friend Haeften and Moltke with whom he made a conspiratorial trip to Norway in spring 1942, without, however, developing closer ties to this resistance group since he was already too

---

[98] See Günter Brakelmann, Dietrich Bonhoeffers Tätigkeit in der Konspiration 1939-1945, in Brakelmann/Jähnichen (eds.), *Stationen und Motive*, 111-159.

[99] Dorothee von Meding, *Courageous hearts: women and the anti-Hitler plot of 1944* (Oxford, 1997), 2.

[100] Christian Gremmels/Heinrich W. Grosse, *Dietrich Bonhoeffer. Der Weg in den Widerstand* (Gütersloh, 1996), 40

[101] See Bethge, *Bonoeffer*, 775-778; see also Brakelmann, *Konspiration*, 142.

deeply involved in practical preparations for the coup in the *Abwe*hr.[102]
In short, Bonhoeffer's activities in the *Abwehr* were directed at removing the Nazi regime, and used political means such as conspiracy to help overthrow Hitler, which makes Bonhoeffer's approach to resistance different from the one of the Confessing Church as a whole.

2.3 Conclusion

In summary, Bonhoeffer's resistance does not clearly fit into the categories of church and political resistance since it embraces elements of both categories, but is in its main characteristics different from each of them. On the one hand, Bonhoeffer's *Widerstand*, as opposed to the resistance of the Confessing Church and like the political resistance, was directed against the Nazi regime in general, pursued political goals and used political means. On the other hand, Bonhoeffer was, unlike representatives of the political resistance, predominantly guided by theological motives. Consequently, characterizing Bonhoeffer's actions after mid-1940 by terms of political resistance such as "liberal-conservative" or "national-conservative" or generally seeing them as political resistance is not adequate since this would ignore his theological motivation, and the importance of his involvement in the Confessing Church.
Regarding his resistance only as part of the church resistance would also be inappropriate, since Bonhoeffer took the decisive step towards direct and active resistance, which the Confessing Church not only failed to do, but also disapproved of. Rather than calling his resistance after 1940 political resistance or saying that he "went into the political resistance", it would be more appropriate to characterize it as a link

[102] Bethge, *Bonhoeffer*, 750.

between political and church resistance. Since it was an extension of the resistance of the Confessing Church without, however, having its approval of it, it is useful and adequate to regard Bonhoeffer's activities after 1940 as an independent category of resistance which I call the theological-political resistance.

This is also justified by the fact that Bonhoeffer viewed the issue of resistance from a theological point of view. Theology was not simply an "academic" issue for Bonhoeffer, isolated from real life, but the eye through which he saw the world and the dimension through which he conceived of it.[103] Bonhoeffer participated in the active resistance as a Christian and theologian. There was no contradiction between his theological reasoning and his actions in the conspiracy. Moreover, his theological thinking did not merely provide him with a subsequent justification for his activities, but made him join the conspiracy, which demonstrates the predominant importance of theological motives for Bonhoeffer's resistance. Hence, Bonhoeffer did not give up or had to give up his Christian convictions in order to take part in the conspiracy. The fact that Bonhoeffer, as a Lutheran theologian, had to answer difficult theological questions on the path to direct action, and thereby had to face different problems from resistance fighters with a predominantly political perspective additionally justifies, in my view, conceiving of his activities as an independent category of resistance.

Furthermore, he regarded his activities as a "*Grenzfall*" himself, and remained, even after he had joined the *Abwehr,* linked to and influenced by the Confessing Church. It is true that Bonhoeffer's relationship to the Confessing Church deteriorated in reaction to its passive attitude towards the Nazi regime. But nevertheless, from the positive relationship in the first years to the negative relationship in the last ones

[103] Dramm, *Einführung*, 9.

Bonhoeffer was influenced by the Confessing Church in his own attitude towards the resistance question. This shows that the Confessing Church as well as theological questions remained Bonhoeffer's reference point in his thoughts about *Widerstand*. The fact that Bonhoeffer reconciled the dichotomy between ecclesiastical confession and political action and, in this sense, also between the church and the political resistance through his theology, which overcame the traditional interpretation of the doctrine of the two kingdoms, makes his approach to resistance a special one. The generalized characteristics of this special approach, i.e. the theological-political resistance, are the following: the resistance activity was predominantly and from the beginning theologically motivated and looked at from a theological perspective, directed at the removal of the Nazi regime and used political means; and the decision to join the active resistance was the result of an involvement in and critical assessment of actions of the Confessing Church. In short, the theological-political resistance can be defined as a theologically motivated opposition to the Nazi regime aimed at its removal and using political means for this purpose.

In the following chapter I argue that the characteristics of the theological political resistance are applicable to the actions of other resistance fighters as well, and verify this thesis' validity by the case study and example of Hans-Bernd von Haeften.

Chapter 3. Hans-Bernd von Haeften's approach to resistance

Hans-Bernd von Haeften (18.12.1905-15.08.1944) is widely neglected in the literature on the German resistance and the Confessing Church, and only considered as one of the members of the Kreisau Circle. While there are several studies on Moltke, Trott and other members of the Kreisau Circle such as Peters and van Husen, there is no large academic study exclusively devoted to Haeften's role in the German resistance, which does scant justice to his importance in the resistance movement. The lack of studies on Haeften is, apart from the scarce availability of sources, probably related to the fact that he did not participate in the three Kreisau meetings of the Kreisau Circle, which does not mean that he did not take part in the preparatory meetings. Also, unlike Moltke and Trott, he did not travel abroad in order to make the Allies aware of the existence of the German resistance.

However, from these facts we should not draw the conclusion that he was a minor figure in the German resistance. Being the deputy director of the Information Department of the Foreign Office from 1940 on, he could not travel abroad on behalf of the German resistance or participate in the three meetings in Kreisau without creating suspicion of the Gestapo. Haeften was actively involved in plotting the coup of 20 July 1944, and contributed to the Kreisau Circle's plans for a post-war Germany and Europe. As one of the highest-ranking civil servants among the resistance fighters he was to become state secretary at the Foreign Office under Ulrich von Hassell designated to become foreign minister after the 20 July coup.[104]

Moreover, analysing Haeften's activities is important in order to be able to understand the relationship between the political resistance and the resistance of the Protestant Church. Haeften was the only member of the Kreisau Circle who was also a member of the Confessing Church.[105] His involvement both in the Confessing Church and the Kreisau Circle as well as the fact that he like Bonhoeffer was one of the few of the Confessing Church who went beyond the Confessing Church's passive attitude towards the Nazi regime make him a perfect case study in this respect.

In the mainstream literature, for instance in the works of Hans Mommsen[106], the Kreisau Circle is without much distinction among its members characterized by categories of political resistance such as "national-conservative" *Widerstand* and is in a general sense subsumed under the political resistance.[107]

Haeften's attribution to the political resistance, however, neglects his role in the Confessing Church and his theological motivation and perspective in general and is therefore inappropriate. While most resistance fighters such as Carl Goerdeler and Ulrich von Hasssell had only indirect relations to the Confessing Church in the spirit of Christian views and traditions, Haeften was actively involved in it.[108] He had a detailed theological knowledge, although he was not a theologian but a diplomat by profession, and was a friend of and corresponded with Dietrich Bonhoeffer and Martin

---

[104] See Auswärtiges Amt (ed.), *Hans-Bernd von Haeften. Zum Gedenken an die Widerstandskämpfer gegen den Nationalsozialismus aus den Reihen des Auswärtigen Dienstes* (Berlin, 2005); see also Joachim Fest, *Plotting Hitler's death. The German Resistance to Hitler 1933-1945* (London, 1996), 386.

[105] Ringshausen, *Widerstand*, 102.

[106] See Mommsen, *Widerstand*, 3-23.

[107] See Steinbach/Tuchel (eds.), *Widerstand*, 6.

[108] Ringshausen, *Widerstand*, 86.

Niemöller. An attribution of Haeften's resistance to the resistance of the Protestant Church would not be correct, either, since his resistance aimed at the removal of the Nazi regime in general and also used political means for this purpose.
In this chapter it is therefore argued that Haeften's *Widerstand* constitutes a link between the political resistance and the resistance of the Protestant Church. Since Haeften went beyond the resistance of the Protestant Church and viewed the issue of resistance from a theological perspective, he is an example of the theological-political resistance described above. To prove the hypothesis that Haeften fulfils the criteria of this category which consist of the theological motivation and perspective, the involvement in the Confessing Church, the goal of overthrowing the Nazi regime and the use of political means for this purpose, the thesis analyses his role in the Kreisau Circle and the Confessing Church, his ideas on the state-church relationship, his theological and political positions, the impact of his theological thinking on his resistance activities and the development of his Christian faith and his attitude towards the assassination question.
After mentioning some basic biographical facts on Haeften in order to provide a chronological framework and some background information the thesis, first, distinguishes his approach to resistance from the political resistance. Since it is unusual and unexpected that someone like Haeften, being a diplomat by profession, was to such a great extent theologically motivated, the religious influences on him, the development of his theology and of his involvement in the Confessing Church are analysed in a first step. In a second step, the impact of his theological thinking and perspective on his resistance activities is shown. Then the thesis outlines the differences between Haeften's approach to resistance and the

resistance of the Protestant Church, and thereby shows that he fulfils the criteria of the theological-political resistance.
The thesis comes to the conclusion that Haeften's approach has more in common with Bonhoeffer's than that of Hassell, Beck or Goerdeler often characterized as "national-conservative" or that of Moltke which Ger van Roon views as "national-liberal" *Widerstand.*[109] Therefore his activities, as in the case of Bonhoeffer, cannot properly be described only by political categories.
My analysis is primarily based on the letters of Haeften, compiled by Barbara von Haeften, which can be found in the *Gedenkstätte Deutscher Widerstand.*[110]

3.1 Short biographical notes

Hans-Bernd von Haeften was born in Berlin on 18 December 1905 as a son of the General Staff officer Hans von Haeften. After the First World War his father became director of the military history section of the national archives in Potsdam, contributing to the historiography of WWI. His mother was the sister of Walther von Brauchitsch, the Commander-in-Chief of the Army from 1938 to 1941.[111]
Hans-Bernd von Haeften studied law in Berlin and Munich and in 1928/29, having passed his first bar examination, went to Trinity College, Cambridge[112] on a student exchange. In

[109] See Ger van Roon, *Resistance to Hitler. Count von Moltke and the Kreisau Circle* (London, 1971); Strohm, *Ethik*, 346.
[110] See Barbara von Haeften, *Aus unseren Briefen 1931-1944*, private edition. All following letters by Hans-Bernd and Barbara von Haeften from which the thesis quotes are from this compilation. The quotations are own translations except when stated that they are also printed in Roon, Resistance.
[111] Meding, *Courageous hearts*, 163.
[112] In the following publications it is mistakenly noted that Haeften studied in Oxford: Ulrich von Hassell, *Die Hassell-Tagebücher* (Berlin, 1988), 548; Auswärtiges Amt (ed.), *Hans-Bernd von Haeften.*

1930 he married Barbara Curtius, the daughter of Gustav Stresemann's successor as foreign minister, Julius Curtius. In April 1933 Haeften joined the Foreign Office after he had worked as secretary general of the Stresemann Foundation.[113]
Haeften was cultural attaché at the Embassy in Copenhagen (1934-1935) and at the German Embassy in Vienna (Oct.1935 to Sept. 1937), in charge of cultural affairs at the Bucharest Embassy (Nov. 1937 to Sept. 1940) and afterwards deputy of the Information Department of the Foreign Office in Berlin (Oct. 1940 to March 1943). Then he worked as the deputy of the Cultural Department of the Foreign Office (April 1943-July 1944).[114]
From 1933 on Haeften belonged to the emerging Confessing Church. He became an active member of the Kreisau Circle and was brought on 15 August 1944, after his arrest on 23 July, before the *Volksgerichtshof* (People's Court). He was sentenced to death and hanged the same day at Plötzensee Prison in Berlin. His brother Werner von Haeften, by profession a company lawyer, joined the German army after the outbreak of WWII. In 1943 after having recovered from a severe wound he had suffered on the eastern front Werner von Haeften became adjutant to Stauffenberg whom on 20 July 1944 he helped to plant the bomb intended to kill Hitler. He was shot the same night at the *Bendlerblock*, the war ministry.[115]

---

[113] Meding, *Courageous hearts*, 163.

[114] Roon, *Resistance*, 52; see also Hans-Bernd von Haeften's curriculum vitae, in Wilhelm Ernst Winterhager, *Moltke-Almanach 1: Die Herkunft der Mitglieder des Kreisauer Kreises* (Berlin, 1984), 131-132.

[115] Peter Hoffmann, *The History of the German Resistance 1933-1945* (Montreal, 1996), 507-508.

3.2 Distinction from political resistance

3.2.1 Development of Haeften's theological thoughts and his commitment in the Confessing Church

Early influences

Apart from his legal studies Haeften heard lectures by pastor Friedrich Siegmund-Schultze who was honorary professor of social pedagogy in Berlin from 1925 to 1933. Siegmund-Schultze, who also influenced Bonhoeffer's theological thinking, contributed to the beginnings of the ecumenical movement and was a founding member and then international secretary of the ecumenical "World Alliance for Promoting International Friendship through the Churches".[116] Through Siegmund-Schultze Haeften received an insight into the churches' efforts for maintaining peace. His interest in ecumenism which remained an important focus of interest of Haeften throughout his life arose at that time.
Haeften's Christian faith was also early shaped by his friendship with Bonhoeffer, the origins of which lay in their childhood since they had shared the same confirmation class. Haeften met Bonhoeffer several times, especially during Bonhoeffer's time as a lecturer at Berlin University in 1931/1932. Meetings between Bonhoeffer and Haeften took also place in 1933 and 1935[117]. As an additional source of influence Haeften regularly heard sermons by Martin Niemöller who was a pastor in Berlin-Dahlem since June 1931.[118]
Haeften did not always agree with Bonhoeffer's views and his strategy in the beginning Church Struggle, which became

[116] Bethge, *Bonhoeffer*, 191.
[117] Barbara von Haeften, *Nichts Schriftliches von Politik* (Munich, 1997), 20.
[118] Ringshausen, *Widerstand*, 89.

evident when he, for example, in mid-October 1933 regretted Bonhoeffer's decision to go to London since "he is actually in Berlin now an indispensable centre of attention."[119] Haeften believed that "a longer stay there will be good for his dreadful view on the state-church relationship", and thought that "this can later become decisively important"[120] This is a criticism of Bonhoeffer's early theological thoughts on the doctrine of the two kingdoms which, in Haeften's view, emphasized too much the boundaries between state and church[121], since Haeften himself, as is shown below, conceived of both realms in a very close relationship. Hence, Haeften hoped that Bonhoeffer's encounter with the Anglican Church would change Bonhoeffer's view on the two-kingdoms doctrine. This letter also indicates that Haeften, very early, expected a conflict between state and church, and shows that he must have discussed these theological issues in previous talks with Bonhoeffer whose importance in the emerging Church Struggle he clearly recognized, and whose decision to go to London he therefore criticised.

The relationship to Bonhoeffer was maintained during Haeften's posting to Copenhagen (1934-1935) since Bonhoeffer went to see him in Copenhagen *en route* to the Danish island of Fanö where he gave an address at an ecumenical conference.[122] It is not clear whether they discussed Bonhoeffer's talk and whether Haeften influenced Bonhoeffer in his preparations, but it is very probable since Bonhoeffer was preoccupied with drafting his lecture for the conference at the time he visited Haeften (beginning of August

[119] Letter of Hans-Bernd von Haeften to his wife, 16.10.1933.

[120] Ibid.

[121] For Bonhoeffer's early thoughts on this matter see Gerhard Ringshausen, Die lutherische „Zweireichelehre“ und der Widerstand im Dritten Reich, *Kirchliche Zeitgeschichte*, 1 (1988), 235.

[122] Bethge, *Bonhoeffer*, 380.

1934).[123] Also, Bonhoeffer narrowed down the topic of the session "The Universal Church and the World of Nations", which had already been decided by an ecumenical conference in April 1934, and spoke about the war threatening the nations, which also corresponded to Haeften's concerns.[124]

Haeften was, from the beginning, on the side of the Confessing Church, and foresaw early the confrontation with the German Christians, which is shown by his comments on the result of the church elections of July 1933. He wrote that "now the separation will probably be unavoidable"[125], meaning the emerging Confessing Church's separation from the German Christians and the Reich Church Government. From 1933 on Haeften belonged with his wife to the "Evangelical Confessing parish of Berlin-Dahlem"[126], and also extended his theological knowledge by reading Luther in the original texts.[127] Within the Confessing Church and with regard to the Confessing Church synod of Dahlem Haeften was like Bonhoeffer a member of the radical wing. This is evidenced by the fact that Bonhoeffer, when he recommended Haeften to church president Koch for the planned ecumenical office of the Confessing Church in June 1935, wrote that Haeften "is very interested in this matter, ready to give up a great deal of time to it and completely on our side."[128] That Haeften was "completely on our side" meant that he supported the wing of the Confessing Church which uncompromisingly supported the decision of "Dahlem" to view the Confessing Church as the only legitimate Protestant Church in Germany, and to break the relations with the Reich Church government.

---

[123] Ibid.

[124] Ringshausen, *Widerstand*, 88.

[125] Haeften to his wife, 25.7.1933.

[126] See Winterhager, *Kreisauer Kreis*, 33-34.

[127] Haeften to his wife, 1.8. 1933.

[128] Bonhoeffer, *Gesammelte Schriften*, I. 226; also printed in Roon, *Resistance*, 53.

The above mentioned statement of Haeften therefore indicates that in 1933 he was generally in line with the Confessing Church's willingness to separate itself from the Reich Church government and to focus on theology in order to keep Christian faith pure.
From 1935 onwards, however, Haeften increasingly distanced himself from the consequences the Confessing Church drew from this approach. Within this context, he severely criticised Hans Asmussen who, in an article[129], had emphasized that the church should not intervene in state affairs. Haeften rejected this view as an expression of "invented and overartificial dogmatics."[130] To Haeften and his wife this view forgot that one "in certain circumstances has to obey God more than the people"[131].

Vienna

Haeften's Christian faith was considerably influenced by his time in Vienna, where he, between October 1935 and 1937, was cultural attaché at the German Embassy which was led by Franz von Papen. From Vienna he observed the church policy of the newly appointed minister for church affairs, Hanns Kerrl, as well as the Niemöller trial but missed "the atmosphere of the great conflict and [...] decisions."[132] For Haeften's development and his theological views on resistance, which are discussed below, his encounter with the Michaels Fraternity and the Catholic Church in Vienna became very important. Through Haeften's friend Herbert Krimm, at that time second pastor in the Vienna Protestant

[129] See Hans Asmussen, Grundsätzliche Erwägungen zur Volkskirche, *Junge Kirche*, 3 (1935), 288-294.
[130] Haeften to his wife, 13.1.1936.
[131] Barbara von Haeften to her husband, 12.12. 1935
[132] Haeften to his wife, 1.1.1936.

"*Stadtkirche*", whom Haeften got to know during his time in Vienna, Haeften learned about the Berneuchener Movement, which had emerged in 1922 from evangelical circles in the youth movement as a result of the dramatic changes after WWI, as well as the Michaels Fraternity which had originated from it in 1931. The Berneuchener Movement and the Michaels Fraternity aimed at finding new ways of spreading the Gospel and of renewing church life, and especially devoted themselves to prayer and liturgy.[133] Haeften took part in the Michaels celebrations in 1937 and wrote "deeply impressed"[134] to Krimm that "I realized that a renewed service […] must be the root of a renewed life of the church."[135]
Moreover, in Vienna Haeften also made contacts with Catholics, for example with the "Hochland Circle"[136], named after the monthly magazine "Hochland", which offered, because of its critical articles, "spiritual" opposition to the Nazi regime from the beginning of the Nazi era until its prohibition in 1941.[137] Haeften's contacts with the "Hochland Circle" seem to have influenced his theological views given that during his time in Vienna the magazine "Hochland" dealt with theological themes[138] which, as is shown below, became very important for Haeften's motivation to join the resistance.

---

[133] See Hans Carl von Haebler, *Geschichte der Evangelischen Michaelsbruderschaft von ihren Anfängen bis zum Generalkonvent 1967* (Marburg, 1975).
[134] Haeften to Krimm, 5.11.1937.
[135] Ibid.
[136] Haeften, *Nichts Schriftliches*, 22.
[137] Konrad Ackermann, *Der Widerstand der Monatsschrift Hochland gegen den Nationalsozialismus* (Munich, 1965)
[138] See, for example, in respect of an apocalyptical interpretations of the Nazi state G. S. Huber, Das vorweggenommene Reich Gottes?, *Hochland*, 34. Jg. (1937) II, 9, 253 ff.; with regard to the idea of a Christian „ordo" see E.J. Vierneisel, Um das Ende des Mittelalters, *Hochland*, 32. Jg. (1935) I, 6, 554 ff.

Bucharest

In November 1937 Haeften was posted to the Embassy in Bucharest where he was responsible for culture and minorities.[139] In Romania he demonstrated his interest in and commitment to church affairs, was influenced in his thoughts about the state-church relationship, and became involved in the Transylvanian Church Struggle.

A large German minority lived in the Romanian region of Transylvania (German: *Siebenbürgen*).[140] The *Siebenbürgen* Church was closely linked to and intertwined with the German national group since it protected the cultural heritage of the German minority and also represented its interests to the Romanian state authorities, which made a great impression on Haeften.[141]

Since the end of the 1920s the *Siebenbürgen* Nazi movement had encroached into traditionally ecclesiastical fields through parallel structures. The Bishop of the Evangelical Church of the Augsburg Confession in Romania, Viktor Glondys, was at first hesitant to accept the influence of National Socialism on the German minorities in Romania, but after 1936 he and the church were ready to compromise with the National Socialists and recognized their claims for power in view of their increased importance.[142] The conflict between the National Socialist movement and the traditional *Siebenbürgen* forces divided and weakened the *Siebenbürgen* Church and the German minority in Romania, which became a major concern for Haeften during his time in Romania.

---

139 Haeften, *Nichts Schriftliches*, 29.

140 See Wolfgang Miege, *Das Dritte Reich und die Deutsche Volksgruppe in Rumänien 1933-1938* (Frankfurt am Main, 1972), 20.

141 Ludwig Binder, *Die Kirche der Siebenbürger Sachsen* (Erlangen, 1982), 79.

142 Miege, *Volksgruppe*, 212-224.

After the National Socialists had won the majority in the church assembly in July 1938, Bishop Glondys negotiated with the National Socialist church movement "*Völkische Erneuerungsbewegung*" (*Völkisch* Renewal Movement) over its participation in the consistorium, the supreme administrative body of the *Siebenbürgen* Church.[143] This was a decisive church-political change since it paved the way for a coming together of the *Siebenbürgen* Church and the Nazi movement and ideology. This was, according to Haeften, an effort to "incorporate the myth in the Christian faith", and "would [mean] the beginning of a German Christian era."[144] The quotation shows that Haeften considered Nazism and the Christian faith as irreconcilable and that he therefore opposed any attempt to adapt Christianity to Nazi ideology.

However, Haeften believed that the church-political change in Transylvania, in turn, would entail a Confessing Church opposition and hence a Church Struggle in *Siebenbürgen*. He, however, feared that a Church Struggle in Transylvania would threaten the *volkskirchliche* (people's church) orientation of the *Siebenbürgen* Church, i.e. its close links to the German national group and its 800 year-old history, given that in *Siebenbürgen* such a struggle would not have taken place between state authorities and the church, as in the case of Germany, but between ecclesiastical forces and forces within the German ethnic group.[145] His concern about the *volkskirchliche* orientation of the *Siebenbürgen* Church was one reason why he tried to prevent the *Siebenbürgen* Church Struggle.

In his efforts to maintain the links between the *Siebenbürgen* Church and the German national group Haeften was helped by Konrad Möckel who was a pastor in the Transylvanian town

---

[143] Ibid., 252-257.

[144] Haeften to Krimm, 2.2.1938.

[145] Haeften, *Nichts Schriftliches*, 34; Haeften to Krimm, 2.2.1938.

of Braşov (German: Kronstadt).[146] Haeften recognized the decline and rigidity of the church and of the liturgy in *Siebenbürgen* resulting also from the influence of Nazi ideas. He supported Möckel's efforts to transform the "Sunday lectures" into liturgical services in Kronstadt, which Haeften, being influenced by the Michaels Fraternity, believed to be the root for a renewal and reconstruction of the church.[147] In March 1940 Haeften wrote that "Unfortunately, Möckel has a hard time. He is completely alone within the *Siebenbürgen* Church which increasingly moves towards decline and disintegration"[148] and in March 1941 argued that "what is important is the total reconstruction of the ecclesiastical castle."[149]

In these letters Haeften alluded to the *Gleichschaltung* of the *Siebenbürgen* Church and the emerging Transylvanian Church Struggle. He, in the end, could not prevent them, given that Bishop Glondys had to resign under the pressure of the National Socialists and was replaced by the Nazi pastor Wilhelm Staedel, who tried to impose a German Christian orientation on the *Siebenbürgen* Church.[150] However, Haeften also tried to settle the ongoing Transylvanian Church Struggle in that he convinced the leader of the German Evangelical Church's office for external affairs, Bishop Theodor Heckel, in November 1943 to negotiate a truce between the church opposition and the National Socialist church leaders in *Siebenbürgen*.[151]

---

[146] See Ludwig Binder, *Konrad Möckel und die Siebenbürger Sachsen* (Munich, no date mentioned), 39.

[147] See Haeften, *Nichts Schriftliches*, 35; Haeften to Krimm, 5.12.1938.

[148] Haeften to Krimm, 1.3.1940.

[149] Haeften to Krimm, 19.3.1941.

[150] Ulrich Andreas Wien, Victor Glondys, in Betz (ed.), *Religion in Geschichte und Gegenwart*, III. 1011.

[151] Friedrich Müller, *Erinnerungen. Zum Wege der siebenbürgisch-sächsischen Kirche 1944-1964* (Cologne-Weimar-Vienna, 1995), 357.

As far as Haeften's attitude to the Confessing Church is concerned: While Haeften at his time in Berlin saw the necessity of the separation of the Confessing Church from the official Reich Church government and the German Christians in order to keep Christian faith pure, he now with regard to the situation in *Siebenbürgen* fought for maintaining the links between the German ethnic group and the *Siebenbürgen* Church. Consequently, Haeften moved away from the Confessing Church's approach to give up the Protestant Church's *volkskirchliche* (people's church) orientation, i.e. its pretence to covering most parts of the German population and its close links to it.[152] Hence, Haeften's experience with the *Siebenburgen* Church strengthened his view that the sharp distinction between state and church was a naïve one, given that, not only in Romania but also in Germany, the churches, as social groups, were in such a way intertwined with social functions and questions that they were not distanced from political events.

Haeften's new view on this matter was also reflected by the fact that he praised Paul Schütz's criticism of dialectical theology which had been developed by Barth after WWI.[153] Schütz criticised dialectical theology, which, in a nutshell, argued that knowledge of God could not be gained through human reason and stressed the distinction between the human and the divine, since he regarded it as too orthodox, dogmatic and distanced from the people.[154]

During his time in Bucharest Haeften also made contact with the Orthodox Church of Romania. He was impressed by "its ecclesiastical tradition" and by the Orthodox "criticism of our

[152] Information given to the author by Professor Gerhard Ringshausen in an interview on 10 April 2006.

[153] Haeften to Krimm, 4.11.1938.

[154] See Paul Schütz, *Warum ich noch Christ bin* (Berlin, 1937), 190-197.

bureaucratic paralysis of the priest office."[155] In talks with the theologian Nicifor Craini he sought clarity in church-political and especially theological questions and wanted to translate the book "*Les Religions de l'Orthodoxie*" by S. Boulgakoff into German as well.[156]

In September 1940 Haeften was recalled from the Bucharest Embassy since, according to his wife, the NSDAP wanted the work on the German minorities to be done by someone loyal to the party line.[157] However, Haeften remained interested in Balkan affairs. For example, in 1941 he sought to get Krimm posted as a military pastor to *Siebenbürgen* in order to support Möckel and his Michaels Fraternity. Krimm, as a result of Haeften's efforts, was sent as a military pastor to Sofia from where he could help Möckel in *Siebenbürgen.*[158]

Also, in November 1943 he made a trip to the Balkans in order to prepare an official report for the Foreign Office on the German policy towards the Balkan Orthodox Churches, in which he argued for a new orientation of the German policy towards the Orthodox Churches in the conquered or allied Balkan countries. Haeften demanded recognition of the Orthodox Churches as public order powers and pointed out that a "positive attitude to the Balkan Orthodoxy" would be necessary for a rapprochement of the Balkans states to Germany.[159] According to Haeften, the ecumenical trends of the Balkan Churches had to be supported and the Reich had to be ready to become the political protector of the Balkan Orthodoxy. Haeften continued that Russia would take over Germany's role if Germany missed its chance. Moreover, he

---

[155] Haeften to Krimm, 1.1.1940.

[156] Haeften, *Nichts Schriftliches*, 78.

[157] Ibid., 40.

[158] Ibid., 69.

[159] Hans Bernd von Haeften, Aufzeichnungen zur Frage der deutschen Politik gegenüber der Balkan-Orthodoxie, 8.11.1943, PA, AA, Inland I D, R 98794, Anlage.

emphasized that a new German policy towards the Balkan Orthodoxy could only be successful if this foreign-political issue was guarded against interference from the German church policy, i.e. the Church Struggle.[160] The report shows how Haeften's religious and theological interests, especially his warm sympathy, which he had as an ecumenical Christian towards the life of the Orthodox Churches in south-eastern Europe, and his efforts to keep the Church Struggle and Nazi propaganda at a distance from the Balkans, and particularly *Siebenbürgen*, influenced his political assessments and were linked to them.

In summary, Haeften's theological development and the influences he was exposed to have the following characteristics: Haeften was, inter alia, through his friendship with Bonhoeffer and Niemöller, from the beginning, theologically interested and influenced. He did not become religious like Moltke only after having endured many years of the Nazi regime. Since the end of the 1920s he had developed, thanks to Siegmund-Schultze, an interest in the ecumenical cause, which he again showed and practiced during his postings to Vienna and Bucharest, where he sought contacts with the Catholic and the Orthodox Church, respectively. Moreover, Haeften saw the necessity of a renewal of church life and within this context was influenced by the Berneuchener Movement and the Michaels Fraternity.

He committed himself to the Confessing Church from 1933 on and supported its approach of "separation". During his time in Romania, however, we can discern a new attitude of Haeften towards the Confessing Church's actions as a result of his experience with the *Siebenbürgen Volkskirche*, with its deep links to the German minority and its social responsibility, and the problem of separating the church from political developments in *Siebenbürgen*. This experience made him

[160] Ibid.

criticise the Confessing Church's dissociation from the *Volkskirche* concept and its adaptation to a sectarian concept of church, and made him further develop his thoughts about the state-church relationship which he had expressed as early as 1933, when he had expressed criticism of Bonhoeffer's early view on the same matter. Moreover, while Haeften seemed to have favoured, or at least approved, the Confessing Church's "confessing approach" during his time in Berlin, he developed a critical view on this issue in Romania.

3.2.2 Theological motivation for resistance

As in the case of Bonhoeffer, Haeften's disappointment with the Confessing Church's passive attitude made him look for other forms of resistance, and hence became one reason for him to join the Kreisau Circle.

After the November 1938 pogrom ("*Kristallnacht*"), for example, Haeften complained in a letter to Krimm about "the passive attitude of the churches", directing his criticism to the Berneuchener Movement and the Confessing Church and making clear that he disagreed with the Confessing Church's strategy of focusing on confessional work.[161] He wrote with regard to the persecution of the Jews which particularly disturbed him that[162]

> The passive attitude of the church on this matter seems to me to resemble a parson who, while reading piously in the Gospel (he has turned to Luke 10.25 [the story of the Good Samaritan]), loses his way and, immersed in the text, walks on; or as if suffering was so near to his feet

[161] Haeften to Krimm, 5.12.1938.

[162] Roon, *Resistance*, 53.

> that he stumbles over it, and on seeing it retreats to a psalm of comfort to fortify him.[163]

Haeften discussed the question of whether the church could exempt itself from the world of politics in May 1941 in a letter to Krimm containing Haeften's basic theological thoughts on this and other issues. This letter offers a good insight into Haeften's motivation for his decision to join the resistance, since it was written at the time Haeften joined the Kreisau Circle, and thus the active resistance. In this letter Haeften argued that the escalation of the ongoing war destroyed the existence of occidental Christendom, and that the war was not war anymore but murder.[164]

> It is really Christian salvation which is at stake [...]. The church's task would be to call upon the "Christian" soldiers and urgently to warn them against destroying the foundations of any order by ignoring God's inviolable commandments and converting the *corpus christianum* into a *corpus diabolicum*. That up to now there has not been such an appeal is a bad sign of the spiritual impotence of the churches in the face of the demonical possessions of this world. Here is a denial of the message, refutation of the existence of Christendom altogether.[165]

Haeften justified this view with theological arguments, and especially with a criticism of Luther's two-kingdoms doctrine. In the letter to Krimm Haeften conceded that the church "cannot make politics on its own." But a clear separation between state and church was also impossible for him "since

[163] Haeften to Krimm, 5.12.1938; also printed in Roon, *Resistance*, 53-54.
[164] Haeften to Krimm, May 1941; the following quotations in this paragraph are also from this letter; see also Ringshausen, *Widerstand*, 90.
[165] Ibid.

both institutions have to deal with the same people, and since these people cannot, and must not, split the unity of their person into citizen and Christian." Hence, Haeften criticised Luther's distinction between person (*Christperson*), i.e. the Christian in his private life, and office (*Weltperson*), i.e. the Christian holding a public office, and conceived of both kingdoms as areas which could overlap and thereby force to make decisions. "There can be events or situations" – according to Haeften – "which threaten the spiritual salvation, if politics put the citizens in situations for which they cannot take responsibility. Then it comes to those crosspoints or intersections of church and state, which, often and inevitably, demand [...] a decision." Then the church must not "be silent like a dumb dog", but the pastoral duty requires it "to speak, to preach and to admonish." These theological thoughts made Haeften convince that the church had to speak openly against the Nazi regime. Haeften also realized that as a Christian it was his responsibility to work towards the overthrow of the regime. This becomes evident in the following part of his letter to Krimm.

In this letter Haeften also offered the criticism that Protestantism lost the awareness that all earthly things are also contained in an "ordo" which Augustine described as the "*civitas dei*". Haeften argued that Catholicism had better preserved this idea than Protestantism since

> Lutheranism's (not Luther's) resigned acceptance of the fact that the world is of the devil has in fact allowed the world to fall into the hands of the devil. Allowed to slip away by the Church, the world has made itself independent and derives its order of values from itself.[166]

[166] Also printed in Roon, *Resistance*, 54.

We can see that Haeften – probably influenced by his contacts with the Michaels Fraternity and the Catholic and the Orthodox Church – comes close to thoughts about a comprehensive and unitarian "*corpus christianum*" of an Augustinian-medieval ordo, i.e. a community of Christians guided by Christian values in its politics, economics and social life.[167] For Haeften these thoughts seem to have been exemplary and indicative of how Christendom shall fulfil its social responsibility. Within this context, Haeften also pointed out that the highest aim of politics was "to serve the growth of the kingdom of God through earthly order"[168] He, however, argued, despite these thoughts, that Catholicism had drawn from this Augustinian view the wrong conclusion that it could "qua church once and for all develop binding social and state doctrines." According to Haeften, instead, putting Christian faith into concrete terms in the earthly realm is the task of the earthly institutions and always takes different forms according to the changing historical circumstances. Haeften, hence, draws the conclusion that the Christian statesman shall ask the church for advice for his tasks "which are after all given by no other […] than the one Lord."

> If today the question is ever-increasingly posed of whether the development of state and society since about the Renaissance was a wrong track, corresponding to the falling away towards secularizing ideologies at that time […], the homo politicus then should be able to ask the theologian about the possibility of concrete application of Christian insights to the tasks of the orders of human life (from the family to the international system) here and now.[169]

[167] Ringshausen, *Widerstand*, 90.
[168] Haeften to Krimm, May 1941.
[169] Ibid.

From these quotations we can, first, draw the conclusion that Haeften was disappointed by the church resistance and that he wanted to go beyond it. Second, he wanted Christian standards to be applied to politics and to his own professional actions and life, given that Haeften conceived of the two kingdoms as being in a very close relationship, and given that he criticised the distinction of Lutheranism between person and office. Third, Haeften was convinced that Christian principles had to be applied concretely to specifically existing situations. Hence, his belief that Christian values have to be concretely applied to the earthly realm and his determination to uphold these values in general seem to have been one major reason for his resistance.

However, as is shown below, when it came to the question of how to resist and what means to use in respect of the planned coup, Haeften came into conflict with his faith. Hence, his theological perspective and religious faith motivated Haeften to resist and made him doubt the appropriate means of resistance at the same time, which created a tension between obedience to "God's inviolable commandments"[170] and the assumption of responsibility as a result of a challenge to these commandments.[171] In the author's view, Haeften's conviction that Christian faith has to be applied not in abstract terms but in practice and concretely, based on the changing historical circumstances, made him at least temporarily overcome and ease his doubts about the appropriate means of resistance and the tension he was exposed to.

An additional theological motivation for Haeften was his attitude towards divine grace. Unlike Luther and also unlike Bonhoeffer, he did not believe "that grace seizes a person as a passivly condoning one. It is and remains a matter of the man

[170] Quotation from ibid.

[171] See also Ringshausen, *Zweireichelehre*, 243.

to seize the offered grace […]. Grace [is] never only a gift but always task and challenge at the same time."[172] This statement also indicates that Haeften from his theological reasoning about divine grace came to the conclusion that active resistance – which he saw as a challenge – and not passive behaviour was required.

Moreover, like Bonhoeffer, Haeften interpreted the Nazi regime and Hitler in a satanic and apocalyptical way. In this respect the influence of the Michaels Fraternity on Haeften is immense and gives Haeften's approach a particular character. For example, he wrote to Möckel that Michael

> […] Is not only a call of the one who sends him as his angel but at the same time a powerful call of the German past to the German present, which to leave unheeded would mean to escape our innermost vocation. As far as the future of our nation is concerned, everything hangs on whether or not we become increasingly aware of the figure of Michael and his opponent in and above the ruins of the great battlefield.[173]

Moreover, in a letter to Krimm, who was to become a military chaplain, Haeften shortly after the beginning of WWII considered how difficult it was

> […] To credibly remind the soldiers verbis et operis that there is above and beyond the visible front line a totally different invisible battlefield […]. In this bigger fight – the fight of Michael – […] even the most powerful peoples' wars are only partial combats whose sense and importance in the divine plan of action the persons

[172] Haeften to Hannes Brockhaus, January 1941.

[173] Haeften to Möckel, 23.12.1938; also printed in Roon, *Resistance*, 55.

> immediately involved will probably hardly ever understand.[174]

In a letter to the widow of a friend of his from Vienna Haeften wrote that "the apocalyptical pictures are again reality, we are put before the last things by firm hand".[175]
Also, before the People's Court where Haeften was tried together with Trott, Egbert Heyessen and Count Helldorf on 15 August 1944 in the third trial for the 20 July plot, he replied, after having been asked by Freisler what, as a Christian, his attitude was towards the oath to the *Führer*, that

> The view I hold of the world-historical role of the *Führer* is that he is a great executor of evil [German: *Vollstrecker des Bösen*].[176]

The quotations from Haeften's letters and his remark before the People's Court are clear allusions to the situation of Germany under the Nazi regime, and to Hitler who is characterized by Haeften as the opponent of Michael and thus as Satan. Hence, Haeften puts the Nazi regime into an apocalyptical and therefore theological context, and considers the fight against National Socialism a religious one.
Moreover, in his farewell letter to his wife, which he wrote shortly before his execution, Haeften interpreted his own resistance activities in a theological way and made clear that he was guided by theological motives. Haeften, from his theological point of view, came to the conclusion that he in

---

[174] Haeften to Krimm, 29.9.1939.

[175] Haeften to Wilhelm Wolf's widow in an attachment to Haeften's letter to Krimm, 29.9.1939.

[176] Barbara von Haeften, *Aus unserem Leben 1940-1950*, private edition (Heidelberg, 1974).

fact did not observe God's laws by consenting to the assassination:

> "To observe God's laws and to exercise His love and to walk humble with your God"[177]: That is the rule which I have violated. I have not kept the fifth commandment – though shall not kill! (although I once pulled back Werner with it[178]) and have not taken seriously enough the rule of the "quietness and trust."[179] [...] I have done this all in the view and the wish to do right before God.[180]

The letter shows that during his resistance Haeften permanently asked himself whether his actions were in accordance with God's will, and that he committed himself to the resistance in order "to serve the growth of the kingdom of God."[181] His resistance can, in his own perception, therefore be understood as a search for God's will and for how Christian faith is to be applied to daily life. His conclusion that he did not obey God's will refers, in the author's view, to his involvement in the assassination attempt and not to his involvement in the resistance as such since he explicitly speaks about the fifth commandment in his farewell letter. The farewell letter also shows that, until the end of his days, Haeften applied the strict standards of his theology to the 20 July plot, and analysed it within his theological framework, refraining from characterizing the 20 July plot as a political "symbol" or by other political categories.

---

[177] Micah 6.8.

[178] Haeften refers to a dispute with his brother Werner about the assassination question which is analysed below.

[179] Isaiah 30.17.

[180] Hans-Bernd von Haeften, farewell letter to his wife, in Haeften, *Nichts Schriftliches*, 90.

[181] Haeften to Krimm, May 1941.

In summary, Haeften's theology constitutes the background and the foundation of Haeften's way to active resistance and of his efforts to link Christian faith to direct action against the Nazi regime.

Haeften's theology and his approach to *Widerstand* changed over time. In 1933/1934 he agreed with Barth's and the emerging Confessing Church's "confessing approach". During his time in Vienna and Bucharest and through discussions with the theologians Krimm and Möckel, his contacts with the Catholic and the Orthodox Church, as well as the Michaels Fraternity, and his encounter with and commitment to the *Siebenbürgen* Church Haeften, however, came to a view which rejected the Confessing Church's focus on confessional work and which demanded an active role of the church in politics. These insights corresponded to Haeften's development of a less doctrinaire theology emphasizing that Christian faith had to be concretely applied to the real world, and to a theology which, in contrast to Bonhoeffer's early thoughts, did not emphasize the boundaries between state and church. Also, this development brought Haeften to a "political ethic", which he outlined, inter alia, in his letter to Krimm of May 1941, and which demanded a warning of the church against National Socialism, interpreted the Nazi regime in an apocalyptical way, and emphasized that each man had to actively seize the offered grace and would not receive it by a passive attitude.

Haeften's view of grace and of the state-church relationship, as well as his apocalyptical interpretation of the Third Reich, provided him with the general motivation to reject and resist the Nazi regime. At the same time, however, Haeften's theological reasoning, as is pointed out below, made him doubt how to resist and what means to use. Until his death Haeften endured the tension between "God's inviolable commandments"[182] and ethical challenges, between obedience to faith and responsibility, and in more general terms between doctrinaire and more liberal theological thoughts.[183] It was Haeften's development of a less doctrinaire theology and his insight that Christian faith had to be put into concrete terms based on the actual historical circumstances, which allowed him to at least temporarily overcome his doubts about the theological legitimacy of the assassination attempts.

This shows that, as in the case of Bonhoeffer, Haeften could not base his resistance activities directly and without problems on existing theological arguments, but that he had to develop far-reaching theological thoughts and a political ethic, and had to overcome and ask himself difficult theological questions. In any case, however, as for Bonhoeffer's resistance there was a theological motivation for Haeften's. Haeften at no time abandoned his Christian faith but developed his theology corresponding to the demands and the situation of the time in which he lived, and based his decision to resist on his theology.

Hence, since Haeften's participation in the *Widerstand* predominantly arose out of his religious and theological convictions, and out of an involvement in and critical assessment of the Confessing Church, and since he put his resistance activities in relation to his theological thoughts, Haeften fulfils the theological-political resistance criteria of the theological perspective and motivation, and involvement in the Confessing Church.

Certainly, Haeften and Bonhoeffer were also influenced by political considerations and other factors in their rejection of the Nazi regime. Both, for example, opposed the destruction of the rule of law in Nazi Germany. Haeften was against the

---

[182] Quotation from ibid.

[183] Ringshausen, *Zweireichelehre*, 243.

Austrian *Anschluss*[184] and commented on the occupation of the remaining Czech territory in 1939 with the words that "the map of Europe is changed again, not for the last time" and that "the political consequences of this step, especially with regard to the imponderables, are hardly foreseeable for the future."[185] Also, according to his colleague in the Foreign Office, Carl August Zapp, Haeften was against the invasion of Russia.[186]

Moreover, Bonhoffer's and Haeften's familiy background and education predisposed them to conservative attitudes. Bonhoeffer, for example, promoted in *Ethics* some elitist-authoritarian attitudes.[187] Haeften, for instance, believed that Germany should not opt either for the West or the East but, instead, should pursue an independent policy between the East and the West because of its central geographical position, and also expressed some conservative views in his above mentioned Balkan memorandum.[188]

However, it would be wrong therefore to attribute the actions of Haeften and Bonhoeffer to the "national-conservative" *Widerstand* for the following reasons:

First, Bonhoeffer and Haeften were in general neither national in the sense of preserving German ascendancy in Europe, and of not looking beyond Germany's borders, nor conservative in the sense of being inseparably bound to past situations or to a past hierarchy of power. This is demonstrated in the case of Haeften by, for example, his rejection of a Greater Germany indicated by his disapproval of the *Anschluss*, the occupation of the Czech territory and the invasion of Russia as well by his dismay at Nazi antisemitism, and in the case of Bonhoeffer by

---

184 Haeften, *Nichts Schriftliches*, 35.

185 Haeften to Krimm, 15.3.1939.

186 Aufzeichnungen von Freunden und Bekannten, PA, AA, Dokumentationsband "Hans-Bernd von Haeften", 94.

187 See Dramm, *Einführung*, 155.

188 Anton Böhm, Hans-Bernd von Haeften. Eine Skizze, circa 1946, in Haeften, *Nichts Schriftliches*, 68.

his ecumenical ideas and contacts, his commitment to the Jews and his willingness to accept Germany's undconditional surrender.

Second, and more importantly, their political ideas were important factors in their decision to reject the National Socialist state. Their determination to resist, however, and not merely to reject the Nazi regime, was, as shown above, primarily a result and consequence of theological and not of political reasoning, since it did not arise out of a political basic attitude – regardless of whether a liberal, socialist or conservative one – but out of theological thoughts which emphasized the responsibility of Christians and the concrete application of Christian principles in the real world. Within this context, political concerns about, for example, the loss of influence of the traditional elite or the loss of Germany's great power status caused by Hitler's policy, which were of primary importance for resistance fighters such as Carl Goerdeler and Ludwig Beck, did not play a significant role in Bonhoeffer's and Haeften's motivation. Also, with regard to the appropriate means of resistance, as is shown in the following chapter, Bonhoeffer and Haeften were not guided by political opportunism but, again, by their theology. Against this background any exclusively political characterization of Haeften's and Bonhoeffer's resistance would be inappropriate since it would neglect the theological dimension of their resistance.

3.3 Distinction from resistance of the Protestant Church

Like Bonhoeffer's approach to resistance, Haeften's approach is also distinct from the resistance of the Protestant Church since Haeften's actions aimed at the removal of the Nazi regime and used political means for this purpose.

Haeften's rejection of the National Socialist state was fundamental and started from the beginning of the Third Reich. Even before the "seizure of power" Haeften worked together with his friend Kurt Hahn, the founder of the boarding school at Salem, against Hitler's assumption of power.[189] Throughout his entire career Haeften refused to become a member of the NSDAP and dissociated himself from Nazi goals and methods.[190]

It is true that Haeften served the Nazi state and thus a criminal regime as a civil servant. However, Haeften was, according to his wife, very depressed about this fact and often thought about resigning from his office.[191] During his research the author could not find any single document by or about Haeften in the Political Archive of the Foreign Office[192], the collection of his letters or the writings of the Kreisau Circle[193], which would suggest that Haeften supported or identified with any Nazi goal or attitude. From this fact we can draw the conclusion that his decision to stay in office could not be caused by an agreement with, for example, Hitler's goal of achieving German hegemony in Europe, but must have been a result of tactical considerations, i.e., for example, the chance to meet people with the same views and the opportunity to use his official position and his contacts for the *Widerstand*. Moreover, Haeften also seemed to be convinced by his wife's argument that staying in a concentration camp was no alternative,[194] which seems to correspond to Bonhoeffer's reasoning that in view of the given situation "every available alternative seemed equally intolerable, repugnant, and futile

---

[189] Roon, *Resistance*, 52.
[190] Ibid.
[191] Haeften, *Nichts Schriftliches*, 40.
[192] See Personalakte "Hans-Bernd von Haeften", PA, AA.
[193] Documents, in Roon, *Resistance*, 287-386.
[194] Interview with B. von Haeften, in Meding, *Courageous hearts*, 152.

[…]."[195] Likewise, Bonhoeffer also did not work for the *Abwehr* to serve or cooperate with the National Socialists, but to have a disguise for his conspirational activities and to help overthrow the Nazi regime. Hence, Haeften and Bonhoeffer are not examples of the "entente" between traditional German elites and the Nazi leadership, which, according to Klaus-Jürgen Müller, was a main characteristic of the history of the "national-conservative" *Widerstand*.[196]

After Haeften's return to Berlin from Bucharest in October 1940 he soon made contact with the active resistance which he joined, as shown above, predominantly as a result of his disappointment with the Confessing Church's passive attitude and of his theological thoughts. Haeften worked closely together with Adam von Trott zu Solz in the Information Department of the Foreign Office, met there Gottfried von Nostitz, whom he had known from his time at the Vienna Embassy, and joined the resistance circle in the Foreign Office. This resistance circle comprised, apart from Trott and Nostitz, among others Albrecht von Kessel and Erich and Theo Kordt, and was provided cover by State Secretary Ernst von Weizsäcker. In May 1941 Haeften joined the Kreisau Circle after he had been introduced by Trott and Nostitz to Peter Graf Yorck von Wartenburg.[197] Moreover, also in May 1941 Haeften got to know Ulrich von Hassell at his uncle's Walther von Brauchitsch[198] with whom Haeften maintained close contact[199], most likely trying to convince him to join the active resistance – however, given Brauchitsch's indecisive attitude, without success.

---

[195] Dietrich Bonhoeffer, After ten years, in Bonhoeffer, *Letters*, 2.
[196] See Klaus-Jürgen Müller, *Über den militärischen Widerstand*, in Steinbach/Tuchel (eds.), *Widerstand*, 268.
[197] Haeften, *Nichts Schriftliches*, 47.
[198] Hassell, *Hassell-Tagebücher*, 249.
[199] See Haeften's letter to his wife, 21.8.1940.

Haeften contributed to the development of the Kreisau Circle's plans for a post-war Germany and Europe. For example, according to Ger van Roon, Moltke's 1941 memorandum "Starting point, aims and problems"[200] was considerably influenced by his conversations with Trott and Haeften.[201] Although he could not participate in the three Kreisau meetings of May and October 1942 and June 1943 because of his fear of arousing suspicion of the Gestapo and also because of health problems, he took part in the preparatory meetings and contributed especially to the Kreisau Circle's planning for post-war German foreign policy, questions of the constitutional and social order and of church policy. After the war Haeften's friend from his time in Vienna, Anton Böhm, gave an account of how much Haeften shared the Kreisau Circle's views.[202] According to Böhm, Haeften demanded a just social order with the preservation of individual freedom. For Haeften, democracy, which he favoured in a socialist form for a post-war Germany, was a consequence of earnest Christendom because of the importance it attached to the individual. Böhm also pointed out that Haeften believed that democracy for Germany also had to take a federal form, while he regarded in foreign policy the establishment of universal peace as the major objective since he saw in peace a Christian task.[203] Haeften's democratic attitude was confirmed by his colleague in the Foreign Office, Wilhelm Melchers. According to him, Haeften wanted Germany's authoritarian system to be transformed into a democratic one.[204]

---

[200] Printed in Roon, *Resistance*, 317-328.
[201] Ibid., 112.
[202] Böhm, *Haeften*, 64-68.
[203] Ibid.
[204] Aufzeichnungen von Freunden und Bekannten, PA, AA, Dokumentationsband "Hans-Bernd von Haeften", 61.

Haeften also played an important role in the attempts of the Kreisau Circle and the German resistance movement to establish contact with the Allies. In May 1942 Haeften briefed Hans Schönfeld and Bonhoeffer before their meeting with Bishop Bell about the Kreisau Circle's plans and ideas. Moreover, Haeften assisted Bonhoeffer with his travels abroad and helped coordinate Trott's journeys to neutral countries in the last years of WWII.[205]

After Moltke was arrested in January 1944, Haeften became actively involved in the preparations for the coup of 20 July 1944, and in the coup itself. He was on hand in Berlin with Hassell and Trott on the same day, ready to seize control of the Foreign Office.[206] These facts show that Haeften committed himself to the removal of the Nazi regime and contributed to the attempts to overthrow it. Hence, Haeften differs in a substantial point from the resistance of the Protestant Church which was confined, as demonstrated above, to more limited goals. Therefore, he fulfils the theological-political resistance criteria of a resistance activity directed at the removal of the Nazi regime.

Haeften, however, under the influence of his more doctrinaire theology of 1933, remained in doubt about the appropriate means to remove Hitler from power. This became evident in the assassination question or in other words the question of tyrannicide, which created a major inner tension in Haeften. Throughout the conspiracy he sought to find an answer to the question of whether or not he could consent to the assassination attempt in his Christian faith.

His attitude to the issue of tyrannicide was based on religious considerations and on grounds of Christian morality.[207] On the one hand, he regarded the method of assassination as offensive

[205] Haeften, *Nichts Schriftliches*, 70-71.

[206] Roon, *Resistance*, 274.

[207] Hoffmann, *Resistance*, 371.

and as a violation of the fifth commandment, and therefore, like Moltke, preferred to try Hitler before a court.[208] On the other hand, he could no longer bear the guilt of not committing himself to the final decision. We see here again the tension between obedience to faith and ethical responsibility Haeften was exposed to.

Haeften asked his brother Werner at the end of January 1944 when the latter thought that he had a chance of making the attempt on Hitler's life himself whether he really saw this as his task. He asked: "Are you sure that this is your mission in the eyes of God and of your forefathers? Can you really take responsibility for this?" As a result of this question Werner backed away.[209] According to Barbara von Haeften, however, her husband was very agonised during subsequent months that he had dissuaded Werner from his plan.[210] Also, at the beginning of July 1944 he took his friend pastor Krimm to one of the final decisive discussions with Yorck, Trott and others, in order to give his Christian arguments greater weight and to seek clarification in this matter.[211] His statement to his brother Werner that "we cannot employ gangster methods"[212] shows that Haeften was, in addition to his belief that the fifth commandment had to be observed, convinced that immoral means could not achieve a morally desired success and something morally good. Also, according to Barbara von Haeften, her husband took the view that tyrannicide was justified only as long as Hitler's star was in the ascendant and believed that "it should have been done before Stalingrad, he should have been killed long ago – if at all."[213] Haeften also

---

[208] Haeften, *Leben*, 13; Haeften, *Nichts Schriftliches*, 83; with regard to Moltke's attitude to the assassination question see Hoffmann, *Resistance*, 371-372.

[209] Interview with B. von Haeften, 154; Haeften, *Nichts Schriftliches*, 81.

[210] Ibid., 154.

[211] Roon, *Resistance*, 273.

[212] Ibid.

[213] Interview with B. von Haeften, 154.

put this view into a theological context since he argued that killing Hitler once the regime was going downhill would not have God's blessing.[214]

Finally, he made up his mind to consent to the attempt on Hitler's life, but again doubted its legitimacy in prison as his farewell letter to his wife indicates. In the author's view, his conviction that Christian insights had to be concretely applied to the tasks of the orders of human life allowed Haeften in the end to agree to the attempt on Hitler's life. Also, Bonhoeffer's reasoning about the assassination may have helped Haeften ease his scruples and doubts. The fact that Haeften consented to the assassination attempt despite his scruples and that he could say that "I have done this all in the view and in the wish to do right before God"[215] suggests a certain closeness to Bonhoeffer's thoughts about responsible life and his insight that responsible action can often only choose between what is relatively good to what is relatively worse, making Haeften an example of Bonhoeffer's concept of a responsible man. This is also indicated by the fact that Haeften's question to his brother as to whether he "can […] really take responsibility for this" is similar to the response Bonhoffer gave Werner von Haeften after he had asked him "Shall I shoot? Do you think, shall I shoot […]."[216] Bonhoeffer answered that

> Shooting is not the problem, the problem is what comes then. Shooting does not make any sense if then there are the next two Hitlers. Our problem is not shooting, our problem is what we will do with the time thereafter so that it will not be worse than before?[217]

---

[214] Ibid.

[215] Haeften, *farewell letter*, 90.

[216] Ringshausen, *Widerstand*, 104-105.

[217] Ibid.; Bonhoeffer probably approved of the assassination attempt at the end of 1941, in summer 1942 at the latest, see Bethge, *Bonhoeffer*, 755.

While Bonhoeffer interpreted the fifth commandment in an orthodox way in *Discipleship*[218], he revised his position in *Ethics* as a consequence of his reasoning about responsible life. He argued that in view of the time thereafter a decision was needed which was ventured in faith, given the disguise of good and evil in the concrete historical situation.[219] Consequently, in a situation of free responsibility, the problem is not anymore the assassination but the responsibility for the future, i.e. how the coming generation is to live. Hence, given that both the acceptance of the Nazi regime and the resistance and the use of violence against it were connected with guilt, and that it was not an absolute good which was to be realized but what was relatively better to what was relatively worse, Bonhoeffer realized, as indicated above, that violent resistance was a free decision taken before and rooted in the belief in God who calls for responsibility and who forgives guilt.

There is a similarity between Bonhoeffer's insight that the point is not to endure something in accordance with abstract principles but in concrete responsibility and Haeften's conclusion that Christian faith has to be concretly applied according to the specific historical situation. In the author's opinion, these views made Bonhoeffer and Haeften – although Haeften had great hesitation and later condemmed his own action – consent to and support the assassination attempt.

In short, Haeften, in the end, consented to, and worked for, the assassination attempt and thus used political means to remove the Nazi regime. He thus fulfils all criteria of the theological-political resistance since his resistance was theologically motivated and was looked at from a theological perspective, was a result and extension of his activities in the Confessing Church, aimed at the removal of the Nazi regime and used for

[218] Bonhoeffer, *Discipleship*, 122.

[219] Bonhoeffer, *Ethics*, 186.

this purpose political means. After having proven that Haeften's resistance is distinct from the political resistance and the resistance of the Protestant Church and that it fulfils the criteria of the theological-political resistance, the thesis therefore concludes that, in summary, he can and should be attributed to this resistance category and not – as has hitherto been done – to the political resistance.

It becomes evident that Haeften's resistance activities were linked to his faith, making his theological perspective, the political means he used and the goals he pursued indistinguishably interlinked. Haeften's *Widerstand* can only be properly analysed and understood if his theological motivation and perspective are sufficiently taken into account. This would, however, not be the case if he were attributed to the political resistance. His difficulty in consenting to the assassination of Hitler and, hence, his lack of "Machiavellianism", for example, could not be explained without the knowledge of his Christian faith as the central motive in his resistance against the Nazi regime.
Even the political resistance which was inter alia religiously motivated cannot, in the author's view, cover his resistance activities for the following reasons. Haeften and Bonhoeffer were actively involved in the Confessing Church unlike political resistance fighters who were also motivated by religious-ethical motives. Their decision to join the active resistance was also a result of their disappointment with the Confessing Church's passive attitude. Hence, their resistance constituted a link between the resistance of the Protestant Church and the political resistance rather than genuine political resistance which was inter alia motivated by religious reasons. This distinction and the emphasis put on Bonhoeffer's and Haeften's involvement in the Confessing Church and in the state-church conflict in Nazi Germany make a big

difference since Haeften and Bonhoeffer, in their active resistance, could build on their experience gained in this conflict and were formed by it. For example, thanks to their involvement in the Confessing Church, Haeften and Bonhoeffer were able to realize that National Socialism was not only a political danger but also a pseudo-religious movement, and were also able to see that conventional means of opposing the Nazi regime such as sending memos to Hitler were ineffective in bringing about a change in Nazi Germany.

Moreover, Haeften was more than simply influenced by Christian faith, since he approached the issue of resistance and its related questions from a scientific-theological perspective. Hence, his *Widerstand* did not arise out of a Christian "emotional" feeling but out of a theological reflection on the issue of resistance. His Christian convictions motivated him, from the beginning of his encounter with National Socialism, to reject and resist the Nazi regime, unlike, for instance Moltke, who became religious only through his resistance. Also, Haeften's theology was not only one factor among others motivating him to resist but the decisive and central one.

This does not suggest that his theology, therefore, predetermined his path to resistance or straightforwardly gave Haeften a justification for his actions. On the contrary, given that the right to resist founded on religion had practically disappeared in Germany by the historical development of German Protestantism, Haeften, like Bonhoeffer, had to develop his own thoughts about political ethics. Both Haeften and Bonhoeffer were initially influenced by orthodox theological positions, as evidenced by Bonhoeffer's positions in *Discipleship* and Haeften's theological scruples about the assassination question. Only gradually did they develop theological thoughts which allowed them to interpret Christian commandments in a less doctrinaire way and to apply them to the actual time and place. Hence, in the case of Haeften and of Bonhoeffer, the critical assessment of a doctrinaire interpretation of Christian principles and of the "confessing approach" contributed to their active resistance.

Also, Haeften remained in doubt about the theological legitimacy of an assassination and – although he finally made up his mind to consent to and support the assassination attempt – believed in prison that he had violated God's laws, which can be interpreted as a resonance of his theology of 1933. Only when considering these fundamental theological problems is it possible to understand Haeften's and Bonhoeffer's way to resistance. This is one reason why introducing the theological-political resistance category is so important: It emphasizes the theological perspective of these resistance fighters. It does not suggest that Haeften and Bonhoeffer could easily find in their faith a justification for their actions and peace of mind, but, on the contrary, aims at highlighting the difficulties and inner tensions these resistance fighters had to endure, since these tensions gave their resistance a particular character which deserves to be analysed as a separate category of resistance. Understanding these tensions is, however, only possible if not only the acts of resistance themselves or their effects are taken into account in an analysis but also, in line with the thesis's approach, the theological "weapons" Bonhoeffer and Haeften developed to cope with the Nazi regime as well as their motives to resist.

Conclusion

The terms "national-conservative" or "liberal-conservative" *Widerstand* which are often used in the academic literature, for example by Hans Mommsen and Klaus-Jürgen Müller[220], to characterize the activities of the Kreisau Circle and the resistance of Bonhoeffer are too imprecise to cover all members of the Kreisau Circle and to describe Haeften's and Bonhoeffer's resistance, since they neglect, because of their political connotation, the theological dimension and motivation of these resistance fighters. The particular character of Bonhoeffer's and Haeften's resistance implies other significant differences to the "national-conservative" and political resistance in general given that Haeften and Bonhoeffer, for instance, even if they did not resist the Nazi regime from 1933 onwards, opposed it from the beginning, did not identify with any single policy or goal of the Nazi regime be it in foreign or domestic policy, and were not guided in their determination to overthrow Hitler by political considerations such as the wish to secure Germany's great power status or to replace Hitler by a more competent leader. In this sense Haeften's and Bonhoeffer's resistance was more fundamental than that of, for example, Beck, Goerdeler or Hassell who had partly cooperated with the Nazis and who had also agreed, or during their resistance still agreed, with some Nazi policies.

There were, certainly, differences between Bonhoeffer and Haeften. For example, they differed in their view on the state-church relationship, since Bonhoeffer especially in his early thoughts emphasized more than Haeften the boundaries between state and church. Also, Bonhoeffer could support more easily than Haeften the assassination attempt. Moreover,

[220] See Müller, *Nationalkonservative Elite*, 24-49; Mommsen, *Widerstand*, 3-23.

while Bonhoeffer in retrospect, i.e. in prison, could say that he acted with a clear conscience[221], Haeften, in his farewell letter, confessed that he had not observed the fifth commandment.[222]
Nevertheless, Bonhoeffer's and Haeften's approach to resistance have in the author's view so many substantial characteristics in common, which are encompassed by the criteria of the theological-political resistance, that it is right to apply the generalized characteristics of Bonhoeffer's approach to resistance to Haeften, hence subsuming Bonhoeffer's and Haeften's activities under one concept of resistance.

First, both resistance fighters were theologically motivated to participate in the active resistance against the Nazi regime, which is demonstrated in many respects. Both Haeften and Bonhoeffer put the Nazi era into a theological context, interpreted it as an apocalyptical appearance and regarded Hitler as a "great executor of evil" (Haeften), the "opponent of Michael" (Haeften), "Satan" (Bonhoeffer) or the "Anti-Christ" (Bonhoeffer), which are all satanic characterizations of Hitler. Bonhoeffer and Haeften reflected on the state-church relationship which became for both a crucial question in their decision to resist. Like Bonhoeffer, Haeften was, to a great extent, influenced by the ecumenical movement and demanded a more active role of the church in opposing Hitler and regarded universal peace as a Christian task and goal. They also have in common that they developed a political ethic and liberal theological thoughts in the sense of a less doctrinaire interpretation of Christian principles as a result of their reasoning about the Nazi regime, which allowed them to take part in the resistance. Within this context, there is a similarity between Bonhoeffer's insight that Christian ethics must be concrete and not abstract and Haeften's conviction that Christian rules have to be applied to the earthly realm and

[221] Bonhoeffer, *Letters*, 174.
[222] Haeften, *farewell letter*, 90.

have to be applied concretely corresponding to the given historical situation. Moreover, Bonhoeffer's ethic of responsible life is similar to Haeften's reasoning about the assassination question and his remarks in his farewell letter which suggest that Haeften perceived the assassination attempt as a venture of faith surrendering the judgement about it to God. In this sense Haeften and Bonhoeffer can be regarded as protagonists of Bonhoeffer's demand for a responsible life.

Second, Haeften and Bonhoeffer were also involved in the confrontation between state and church and the Confessing Church and were critical of its actions. The disappointment with the Confessing Church's passive attitude became one major motive for their *Widerstand*. Hence, their actions can be conceived of as an extension of the church resistance.

Third, both Haeften in the Kreisau Circle and Bonhoeffer in the *Abwehr* were actively involved in the active resistance and aimed at removing the Nazi regime. They participated, in and contributed to, the attempts to overthrow Hitler and also took part in discussions about the reorganization of Germany after the war. Both also contributed to the efforts of the German resistance to make contact with the Allies – Bonhoeffer by travelling abroad and Haeften by preparing memoranda for the Allies.

Fourth, both used political means such as conspiracy and tyrannicide to remove Hitler from power, but also had to endure inner conflicts and tensions as to whether, and to what extent, they could support concrete means of resistance the legitimacy of which they examined from a theological perspective.

Also, their growing-up in an educational and open-minded environment, their international contacts and experiences, their studies abroad, as well as their friendship and relationship with persons from whom they received information on Nazi atrocities (Dohnanyi as regards

Bonhoeffer and Moltke in respect of Haeften) constituted, for both Bonhoeffer and Haeften, similar and favourable, but not necessarily compelling, conditions under which they could become immune from Nazi ideology and under which they could decide to resist the Nazi regime.

In sum, the thesis made the following contribution: First, it pointed out that Bonhoeffer's resistance cannot be attributed to the resistance of the Protestant Church or the political resistance but constitutes an independent category which the thesis calls the theological-political resistance. Second, the thesis found that the generalized criteria of Bonhoeffer's resistance are applicable to Haeften since his resistance is similar to that of Bonhoeffer in many aspects. Third, Haeften should, therefore, not be attributed to the political resistance, as hitherto done in the literature, and not be attributed to the resistance of the Protestant Church because of his participation in the conspiracy, either. Rather, Haeften's and Bonhoeffer's approach to resistance represented, because of its synthesis of, on the one hand, the theological perspective and motives of the church resistance, and, on the other hand, the political means and goals of the political resistance, a theological-political approach, reconciling the dichotomy between the political and the church resistance. Consequently, Haeften's and Bonhoeffer's resistance activities should not be understood as a way from the resistance of the Protestant Church to the political resistance, leaving theology behind them, since their resistance activities cannot be separated from their theology and faith, and since they both did not break with their faith in the resistance but, on the contrary, received their motivation from their understanding of the duty of a faithful Christian.

Fourth, the thesis underlines the importance of Haeften, who is generally neglected in the academic literature on the Confessing Church and in the Kreisau Circle, and also in studies on the relationship between the political resistance and the resistance of the Protestant Church. Fifth, the thesis draws from the above mentioned results the conclusion that it is necessary to analyse and characterize the German resistance in a more discriminating way on the basis of a more detailed analysis of individual biographies of the resistance fighters and their motives to resist.

One might argue that the "labelling" of resistance fighters as such does not make any sense since each resistance fighter was unique both with regard to his or her personality and his or her motivation. However, categorization and generalization are important for historiography and research in general since these methods allow making comparisons and drawing general conclusions, and provide an analytical framework on the basis of which the subject of *Widerstand* in Nazi Germany can be examined.[223] Within this context, describing Bonhoeffer's and Haeften's approach to resistance as theological-political resistance is not only a question of terms but is a way of understanding it and is important for a conception of the character and particularities of their resistance activities.

The thesis focused on Bonhoeffer and Haeften as case studies of the theological-political resistance because of their outstanding importance, and because of limitations of space. However, in the author's view there are also other resistance fighters who can be subsumed under this resistance category such as the legal adviser of the Confessing Church Friedrich Justus Perels and the lawyer and estate owner Ewald von Kleist-Schmenzin, which suggests that a generalization of Bonhoeffer's and Haeften's resistance and its application to the activities of other resistance fighters is possible.

The issues dealt with in this thesis are not only of historical significance. After 1945 there have also been dictatorships and totalitarian regimes which have forced churches and Christians

[223] Müller, *Über den militärischen Widerstand*, 267.

all over the world to ask themselves questions about their attitudes towards confession, resistance and political responsibility. Bonhoeffer's demands for responsible action, concreteness of revelation and his refusal of retreat into privacy have influenced many people in their fight against oppression. For instance, in the struggles against *Apartheid* in South Africa, as well as against dictatorships in Latin America and also in the former GDR, Christians could base their fight on experiences of the Church Struggle and the German resistance in Nazi Germany.[224] Many of these struggles can only be understood if, as in the case of the theological-political resistance, the link between theological motivation and political goals and means are recognized. Bonhoeffer's and Haeften's resistance constitutes a call for an active role and the assumption of responsibility of the churches, Christians and responsible men and women in general, in times of "ultimate necessities"[225], then and now. It remains to be seen whether we can meet their expectations in the future.

---

[224] See John D. Godsey/Geffrey B. Kelly (eds.), *Ethical Responsibility: Bonhoeffer's Legacy to the Churches* (New York, 1981).

[225] Bonhoeffer, *Ethics*, 207.

BIBLIOGRAPHY

Primary Sources

Unpublished

Aufzeichnungen von Freunden und Bekannten, Politisches Archiv des Auswärtigen Amtes in Berlin (PA, AA), Dokumentationsband "Hans-Bernd von Haeften".

Hans-Bernd von Haeften, Aufzeichnungen zur Frage der deutschen Politik gegenüber der Balkan-Orthodoxie, 8.11.1943, PA, AA, Inland I D, R 98794, Anlage.

Personalakte "Hans-Bernd von Haeften", PA, AA.

Published

Akten zur deutschen auswärtigen Politik 1918-1945. Aus dem Archiv des Auswärtigen Amtes, Serie C: 1933-1937 (Göttingen, 1971-1981).

Althaus, Paul, *Das Erlebnis der Kirche* (Leipzig, 1924).

Asmussen, Hans, Grundsätzliche Erwägungen zur Volkskirche, *Junge Kirche* , 3 (1935), 288-294.

Barth, Karl, *Theological Existence* Today (London, 1933).

Barth, Karl, *Theologische Fragen und Antworten, Gesammelte Vorträge* (Zurich, 1957).

Bell, George, The Church and the Resistance Movement, in Bonhoeffer, *Gesammelte Schriften,* I. 399-413.

Bell, George, The background of the Hitler plot, in Bonhoeffer, *Gesammelte Schriften*, I. 390-398.

Böhm, Anton, Hans-Bernd von Haeften. Eine Skizze, circa 1946, in Barbara von Haeften, *Nichts Schriftliches von Politik*, 64-68.

Bonhoeffer, Dietrich, After ten years, in Bonhoeffer, *Letters and Papers from Prison*, 1-17.

Bonhoeffer, Dietrich, Confession of Guilt, in Bonhoeffer, *Ethics*, 89-95.

Bonhoeffer, Dietrich, *Konspiration und Haft 1940-1945*, *Bonhoeffers Werke 16*, edited by Ulrich Katz et al. (Gütersloh, 1996).

Bonhoeffer, Dietrich, *Ethics* (London, 1993).

Bonhoeffer, Dietrich, *Gesammelte Schriften*, edited by Eberhard Bethge (4 vols., Munich, 1956).

Bonhoeffer, Dietrich, *Letters and Papers from Prison*, edited by Eberhard Bethge (New York, 1997).

Bonhoeffer, Dietrich, *No rusty swords: Letters, Lectures and Notes, 1928-1936*, edited by Edwin H. Robertson (New York, 1965).

Bonhoeffer, Dietrich, *Selected Writings*, edited by Edwin Robertson (London, 1995).

Bonhoeffer, Dietrich, The Church and the Jewish Question, in Bonhoeffer, *Selected Writings*, 45-47.

Bonhoeffer, Dietrich, The Church and the new order in Europe, in Bonhoeffer, *Gesammelte Schriften*, I. 362-371.

Bonhoeffer, Dietrich, *The Cost of Discipleship* (London, 1948).

Documents of the Kreisau Circle, in Ger van Roon, *German Resistance*, 287-386.

Gisevius, Hans-Bernd, *Bis zum bitteren Ende* (2 vols., Zurich 1946).

Greschat, Martin (ed.), *Zwischen Widerspruch und Wahrheit. Texte zur Denkschrift der Bekennenden Kirche an Hitler* (Munich, 1987).

Haeften, Barbara von, *Aus unseren Briefen 1931-1944*, private edition (typescript, no place and date mentioned).

Haeften, Barbara von, *Aus unserem Leben 1940-1950*, private edition (Heidelberg, 1974).

Haeften, Barbara von, *Nichts Schriftliches von Politik. Hans-Bernd von Haeften: Ein Lebensbericht* (Munich, 1997).

Haeften, Hans-Bernd von, farewell letter to his wife, in Barbara von Haeften, *Nichts Schriftliches von Politik*, 89-92.

Hassell, Ulrich von, *Die Hassell-Tagebücher*, edited by Friedrich Freiherr Hiller von Gaertringen (Berlin, 1988).

Hirsch, Emanuel, Vom verborgenen Souverän, *Glaube und Volk*, Jg. 2 (1933), 4-13.

Huber, G. S., Das vorweggenommene Reich Gottes?, *Hochland*, 34. Jg. (1937), II, 9, 253 ff.

Interview with Barbara von Haeften, in Dorothee von Meding, *Courageous hearts: women and the anti-Hitler plot of 1944* (Oxford, 1997), 144-165.

Moltke, Helmuth James Graf von, *Briefe an Freya. 1939-1945*, edited by Beathe Ruhm von Oppen (Munich, 1988).

Müller, Friedrich, *Erinnerungen. Zum Wege der siebenbürgisch-sächsischen Kirche 1944-1964* (Cologne-Weimar-Vienna, 1995).

Schütz, Paul, *Warum ich noch Christ bin* (Berlin, 1937).

The Theological Declaration of Barmen (http://www.ucc.org/faith/barmen.htm)

Vierneisel, E.J., Um das Ende des Mittelalters, *Hochland*, 32. Jg. (1935) I, 6, 554 ff.

Secondary Sources

Interviews

Interview with Professor Manfred Gailus.

Interview with Professor Gerhard Ringshausen.

Books and Articles

Ackermann, Konrad, *Der Widerstand der Monatsschrift Hochland gegen den Nationalsozialismus* (Munich, 1965).

Auswärtiges Amt (ed.), *Biographischen Handbuchs des deutschen Auswärtigen Dienstes 1871-1945*, Bd. 2 (Paderborn 2005).

Auswärtiges Amt (ed.), *Zum Gedenken an die Widerstandskämpfer gegen den Nationalsozialismus aus den Reihen des Auswärtigen Dienstes* (Berlin, 2005).

Baranowski, Shelley, *The Confessing Church, Conservative Elites, and the Nazi State* (New York, 1986).

Barnett, Victoria, *For the Soul of the People: Protestant Protest against Hitler* (Oxford, 1992).

Bärsch, Claus-Ekkehard, *Die politische Religion des Nationalsozialismus: Die religiöse Dimension der NS-Ideologie in den Schriften von Dietrich Eckhard, Joseph Goebbels, Alfred Rosenberg und Adolf Hitler* (Munich, 1998).

Bergen, Doris L., *Twisted Cross. The German Christian Movement in the Third Reich* (Chapel Hill 1996).

Besier, Gerhard, Ansätze zum politischen Widerstand in der Bekennenden Kirche- Zur gegenwärtigen Forschungslage, in Schmädecke and Steinbach (eds.), *Der Widerstand gegen den Nationalsozialismus*, 265-280.

Besier, Gerhard, and Ringshausen, Gerhard (eds.), *Bekenntnis, Widerstand, Martyrium. Von Barmen 1934 bis Plötzensee 1944* (Göttingen, 1986).

Besier, Gerhard, Die Bekennende Kirche und der Widerstand gegen Hitler. Einzelbeobachtungen, *Wort und Dienst*, 18 (1985), 197-227.

Besier, Gerhard, Widerstand im Dritten Reich- ein kompatibler Forschungsgegenstand für gegenseitige Verständigung heute?, *Kirchliche Zeitgeschichte*, 1 (1988), 50-68.

Bethge, Eberhard, *Am gegebenen Ort. Aufsätze und Reden 1970-1979* (Munich, 1979).

Bethge, Eberhard, *Bonhoeffer. An Illustrated Biography* (New York, 1979).

Bethge, Eberhard, *Dietrich Bonhoeffer. Christian. Theologian. Man for his Times* (Minneapolis, 2000).

Bethge, Eberhard, Dietrich Bonhoeffer und die Juden, in Ernst Feil and Ilse Tödt (eds.), *Internationales Bonhoeffer Forum 3* (Munich, 1980), 171-214.

Bethge, Eberhard, Dietrich Bonhoeffer und die theologische Begründung seines politischen Widerstandes, in Bethge, *Am gegebenen Ort*, 48-62.

Bethge, Eberhard, Dietrich Bonhoeffers Weg vom „Pazifismus" zur Verschwörung, in Hans Pfeifer (ed.), *Internationales Bonhoeffer Forum 5* (Munich, 1982), 118-136.

Bethge, Eberhard, *Erstes Gebot und Zeitgeschichte. Ausätze und Reden 1980-1990* (Munich, 1991).

Bethge, Eberhard, Widerfahrnisse und Umgang mit dem Widertandskomplex, in Eberhard Bethge, *Erstes Gebot und Zeitgeschichte* (Munich, 1991).

Bethge, Eberhard, Zwischen Bekenntnis und Widerstand. Erfahrungen in der Altpreußischen Union, in Schmädecke and Steinbach (eds.), *Der Widerstand gegen den Nationalsozialismus*, 281-294.

Betz, Hans Dieter (ed.), *Die Religion in Geschichte und Gegenwart: Handwörterbuch für Theologie und Religionswissenschaft* (8 vols., Tübingen, 1998-2005).

Binder, Ludwig, *Die Kirche der Siebenbürger Sachsen* (Erlangen, 1982)

Binder, Ludwig, *Konrad Möckel und die Siebenbürger Sachsen* (Munich, no date mentioned).

Brakelmann, Günther, and Jähnichen, Traugott (eds.), *Dietrich Bonhoeffer- Stationen und Motive auf dem Weg in den politischen Widerstand* (Münster, 2005).

Brakelmann, Günther, Dietrich Bonhoeffers Tätigkeit in der Konspiration 1939-1945, in Brakelmann and Jähnichen (eds.), *Dietrich Bonhoeffer- Stationen und Motive auf dem Weg in den politischen Widerstand*, 111-158.

Broszat, Martin, Resistenz und Widerstand. Eine Zwischenbilanz des Forschungsprojekts, in Martin Broszat et al. (eds.), *Bayern in der NS-Zeit. Herrschaft und Gesellschaft* (6 vols., Munich, 1977-83), IV. 691-709.

Burleigh, Michael, *The Third Reich: A New History* (London, 2000).

Campenhausen, Hans von, and Galling, Kurt (eds.), *Die Religion in Geschichte und Gegenwart* (6 vols., Tübingen, 1957-1965).

Claussen, Regina, and Schwarz, Siegfried (eds.), *Vom Widerstand lernen. Von der Bekennenden Kirche bis zum 20. Juli 1944* (Bonn, 1986).

Dramm, Sabine, *Dietrich Bonhoeffer. Eine Einführung in sein Denken* (Gütersloh, 2001).

Ericksen, Robert P., A Radical Minority: Resistance in the German Protestant Church, in Nicosia and Stokes (eds.), *Germans against Nazism*, 115-136.

Evans, Richard J., *Rereading German history: from unification to reunification, 1800-1996* (London, 1997).

Evans, Richard J., *The Third Reich in power 1933-1939* (London, 2005).

Fest, Joachim, *Plotting Hitler's death. The German Resistance to Hitler 1933-1945* (London, 1996).

Gailus, Manfred, *Protestantismus und Nationalsozialismus. Studien zur nationalsozialistischen Durchdringung des protestantischen Sozialmilieus in Berlin* (Cologne, 2001).

Gerlach, Wolfgang, *Zwischen Kreuz und Davidstern. Die Bekennende Kirche in ihrer Stellung zum Judentum im Dritten Reich* (Hamburg, 1972).

Godsey, John D., and Kelly, Geffrey B. (eds.), *Ethical Responsibility: Bonhoeffer's Legacy to the Churches* (New York, 1981).

Gremmels, Christian, and Grosse, Heinrich W., *Dietrich Bonhoeffer. Der Weg in den Widerstand* (Gütersloh, 1996).

Haebler, Hans Carl von, *Geschichte der Evangelischen Michaelsbruderschaft von ihren Anfängen bis zum Generalkonvent 1967* (Marburg, 1975).

Heckel, Johannes, Widerstand gegen die Obrigkeit. Pflicht und Recht zum Widerstand bei Martin Luther, in Johannes Heckel, *Das blinde, undeutliche Wort ‚Kirche'. Gesammelte Aufsätze* (Cologne, 1964).

Hoffmann, Peter, Motive, in Schmädecke and Steinbach (eds.), *Der Widerstand gegen den Nationalsozialismus*, 1089-1096.

Hoffmann, Peter, *The History of the German Resistance 1933-1945* (Montreal, 1996).

Holloway, James Y. (ed.), *Barth, Barmen, and the Confessing Church today* (Lewiston, 1995).

Holzer, Willibald I., *Politischer Widerstand gegen die Staatsgewalt* (Vienna, 1985).

Hüffmeier, Wilhelm, and Stöhr, Martin (eds.), *Barmer Theologische Erklärung 1934-1984: Geschichte, Wirkung, Defizite* (Bielefeld 1984).

Jähnichen, Traugott, Freie Verantwortung und Zivilcourage, in Brakelmann and Jähnichen (eds.), *Dietrich Bonhoeffer-Stationen und Motive auf dem Weg in den politischen Widerstand*, 89-110.

Klemperer, Klemens von, *German resistance against Hitler: the search for allies abroad, 1938-1945* (Oxford, 1994).

Klemperer, Klemens von, Glaube, Religion, Kirche und der deutsche Widerstand gegen Hitler, *Vierteljahrshefte für Zeitgeschichte*, 28 (1980), 293-309.

Klemperer, Klemens von, Naturrecht und der deutsche Widerstand gegen den Nationalsozialismus, in Steinbach and Tuchel (eds.), *Widerstand gegen den Nationalsozialismus*, 43-53.

Klemperer, Klemens von, Sie gingen ihren Weg ... – Ein Beitrag zur Frage ds Entschlusses und der Motivation zum Widerstand, in Schmädecke and Steinbach (eds.), *Der Widerstand gegen den Nationalsozialismus*, 1097-1106.

Künneth, Walter, *Das Widerstandsrecht als theologisch-ethisches Problem* (Munich, 1954).

Künneth, Walter, Die evangelisch-lutherische Theologie und das Widerstandsrecht, in Europäische Publikation e.V. (ed.), *Die Vollmacht des Gewissens* (Munich, 1956), 164-174.

Maier, Hans, Das Recht auf Widerstand, in Steinbach and Tuchel (eds.), *Widerstand gegen den Nationalsozialismus*, 33-43.

Meding, Dorothee von, *Courageous hearts: women and the anti-Hitler plot of 1944* (Oxford, 1997).

Meier, Kurt, *Der Evangelische Kirchenkampf* (3 vols., Göttingen, 1976-1984).

Miege, Wolfgang, *Das Dritte Reich und die Deutsche Volksgruppe in Rumänien 1933-1938* (Frankfurt am Main, 1972).

Mommsen, Hans, Der Widerstand gegen Hitler und die deutsche Gesellschaft, in Schmädecke and Steinbach (eds.), *Der Widerstand gegen den Nationalsozialismus*, 3-23.

Müller, Klaus-Jürgen, Nationalkonservative Elite zwischen Kooperation und Widerstand, in Schmädecke and Steinbach (eds.), *Der Widerstand gegen den Nationalsozialismus* (Munich-Zurich, 1985), 24-49.

Müller, Klaus-Jürgen, Über den militärischen Widerstand, in Steinbach and Tuchel (eds.), *Widerstand gegen den Nationalsozialismus*, 267.

Nicolaisen, Carsten, *Der Weg nach Barmen. Die Entstehungsgeschichte der Theologischen Erklärung von 1934* (Neukirchen-Vluyn, 1985).

Nicosia, Francis R., and Stokes, Lawrence D. (eds.), *Germans against Nazism: Nonconformity, Opposition and Resistance in the Third Reich: Essays in Honour of Peter Hoffmann* (Oxford, 1990).

Norden, Günther van, Die Barmer Theologische Erklärung und ihr historischer Ort in der Widerstandsgeschichte, in Steinbach and Tuchel, *Widerstand gegen den Nationalsozialismus*, 170-182.

Norden, Günther van, Die Evangelische Kirche und die Juden im „Dritten Reich", *Kirchliche Zeitgeschichte*, 2 (1989), 38-49.

Norden, Günther van, Widerstand im deutschen Protestantismus 1933-1945, in Christoph Klessmann and Falk Pingel (eds.), *Gegner des Nationalsozialismus: Wissenschaftler und Widerstandskämpfer auf der Suche nach historischer Wirklichkeit* (Frankfurt am Main, 1980), 103-125.

Norden, Günther van, Zwischen Kooperation und Teilwiderstand: Die Rolle der Kirchen und Konfessionen- Ein Überblick über Forschungspositionen, in Schmädecke and Steinbach (eds.), *Der Widerstand gegen den Nationalsozialismus*, 227-239.

Nowak, Kurt, Kirche und Widerstand gegen den Nationalsozialismus 1933-1945 in Deutschland, in Carsten Nicolaisen (ed.), Nordische und deutsche Kirchen im 20. Jahrhundert. Referate auf der internationalen Arbeitstagung in Sandbjerg/Dänemark 1981 (Göttingen, 1982), *Arbeiten zur kirchlichen Zeitgeschichte*, Reihe B: Darstellungen, Bd. 13, 228-270.

Pangritz, Andreas, Dietrich Bonhoeffers theologische Begründung der Beteiligung am Widerstand, *Evangelische Theologie*, 55 (1995), 491-519.

Reuter, Hans-Richard, Widerstandsrecht, in Hans Dieter Betz (ed.), *Die Religion in Geschichte und Gegenwart: Handwörterbuch für Theologie und Religionswissenschaft*, VIII. 1522-1527.

Ringshausen, Gerhard, Der 20. Juli als Problem des Widerstandes gegen die Obrigkeit, in Gerd Ueberschär (ed.), *Der 20. Juli 1944. Bewertung und Rezeption des deutschen Widerstandes gegen das NS-Regime* (Cologne, 1994), 191-202.

Ringshausen, Gerhard, Die lutherische „Zweireichelehre" und der Widerstand im Dritten Reich. Zu D. Bonhoeffers Aufsatz „Die Kirche vor der Judenfrage", *Kirchliche Zeitgeschichte*, 1 (1988), 215-244.

Ringshausen, Gerhard, Evangelische Kirche und Widerstand, in Huberta Engel (ed.), *Deutscher Widerstand-Demokratie heute: Kirche, Kreisauer Kreis, Ethik, Militär und Gewerkschaften* (Bonn-Berlin, 1992), 62-117.

Roon, Ger van, *German Resistance to Hitler. Count von Moltke and the Kreisau Circle* (London, 1971)

Rothfels, Hans, *The German opposition to Hitler* (London, 1962)
Ryszka, Franziska, Widerstand: Ein wertfreier oder wertbezogener Begriff?, in Schmädecke and Steinbach (eds.), *Der Widerstand gegen den Nationalsozialismus*, 1107-1116.

Schmädecke, Jürgen, and Steinbach, Peter (eds.), *Der Widerstand gegen den Nationalsozialismus* (Munich-Zurich, 1985).

Scholder, Klaus, *Die Kirchen zwischen Republik und Gewaltherrschaft* (Berlin, 1988).

Scholder, Klaus, *The Churches and the Third Reich* (2 vols., London 1987-1988).

Steigmann-Gall, Richard, *The Holy Reich. Nazi Conceptions of Christianity, 1919-1945* (Cambridge, 2003).

Steinbach, Peter, and Tuchel, Johannes (eds.), *Widerstand gegen den Nationalsozialismus* (Bonn, 1994).

Steinbach, Peter, Der Widerstand als Thema der politischen Zeitgeschichte, in Gerhard Besier and Gerhard Ringshausen (eds.), *Bekenntnis, Widerstand, Martyrium. Von Barmen 1934 bis Plötzensee 1944* (Göttingen, 1986), 11-74.

Steinbach, Peter, Widerstandsforschung im politischen Spannungsfeld, in Steinbach and Tuchel (eds.), *Widerstand gegen den Nationalsozialismus*, 597-622.

Strohm, Christoph, Der Widerstandskreis um Dietrich Bonhoeffer und Hans von Dohnanyi- Seine Voraussetzungen zur Zeit der Machtergreifung, in Schmädecke and Steinbach (eds.), *Der Widerstand gegen den Nationalsozialismus*, 295-313.

Strohm, Christoph, *Theologische Ethik im Kampf gegen den Nationalsozialismus. Der Weg Dietrich Bonhoeffers mit den*

Juristen Hans von Dohnanyi und Gerhard Leibholz in den Widerstand (München, 1989).

Strohm, Christoph, „Zweireichelehre“ und antiliberales Rechtsverständnis bei Bonhoeffer?, *Kirchliche Zeitgeschichte*, 1 (1988), 245-266.

Tödt, Heinz Eduard, Der Bonhoeffer-Dohnanyi-Kreis in der Opposition und im Widerstand gegen das Gewaltregime Hitlers, in Christian Gremmels and Ilse Tödt (eds.), *Internationales Bonhoeffer Forum 7* (Munich, 1987), 205-263.

Tödt, Heinz Eduard, Die Bedeutung von Luthers Reiche- und Regimentelehre für heutige Theologie und Ethik, in Niels Hasselmann (ed.), *Gottes Wirken in seiner Welt* (2 vols., Hamburg, 1980), II. 53-126.

Tödt, Heinz Eduard, Dietrich Bonhoeffers ökumenische Friedensethik, in Hans Pfeifer (ed.), *Internationales Bonhoeffer Forum 5* (Munich, 1982), 85-117

Tödt, Heinz Eduard, Judendiskriminierung 1933- der Ernstfall für Bonhoeffers Ethik, in Wolfgang Huber and Ilse Tödt (eds.), *Internationales Bonhoeffer Forum 4* (Munich, 1982), 139-183.

Tödt, Heinz Eduard, *Komplizen, Opfer und Gegner des Hitlerregimes: zur „inneren“ Geschichte von protestantischer Theologie und Kirche im „Dritten Reich“* (Gütersloh 1997).

Weinkauff, Hermann, Die Militäropposition gegen Hitler und das Widerstandsrecht, in Europäische Publikation e.V. (ed.), *Die Vollmacht des Gewissens* (Munich, 1956), 137-158.

Wien, Ulrich Andreas, Victor Glondys, in Betz (ed.), *Die Religion in Geschichte und Gegenwart*, III. 1010-1011.

Winterhager, Wilhelm Ernst , *Der Kreisauer Kreis. Portrait einer Widerstandsgruppe* (Berlin, 1985).

Winterhager, Wilhelm Ernst, *Moltke-Almanach 1: Die Herkunft der Mitglieder des Kreisauer Kreises* (Berlin, 1984).

Wolf, Ernst, Widerstandsrecht, in Hans von Campenhausen and Kurt Galling (eds.), *Die Religion in Geschichte und Gegenwart*, VI. 1685-1692.

Wolf, Ernst, Zum Verhältnis der politischen und moralischen Motive in der deutschen Widerstandsbewegung, in Schmitthenner, Walter, and Buchheim, Hans (eds.), *Der deutsche Widerstand gegen Hitler* (Cologne, 1966), 215-255.